Kato Kaelin:
The Whole Truth

*The Real Story of
O.J., Nicole, and Kato*

Kato Kaelin:
The Whole Truth

The Real Story of
O.J., Nicole, and Kato

FROM THE ACTUAL TAPES

Marc Eliot

HarperPaperbacks
A Division of HarperCollins*Publishers*

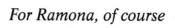

For Ramona, of course

Table of Contents

Acknowledgments

In many ways, writing about the O.J. Simpson trial is like being given a shot at the Great American Novel, except the plot is prefabricated. The characters are a combination of Mailer: great-looking all-American blondes; Fitzgerald: handsome, weak men; Raymond Chandler: hard murder in L.A.; and enough lurid sex to satisfy Henry Miller. Unfortunately, there is no "higher truth of fiction" available, no dramatic dénouement for one of the great stories of modern American love and obsession to crawl that lonesome road of heartbreak and failed dreams. It is, rather, the difference between the character of fate and the fate of characters.

In my life, I place enormous importance on friendship, trust, and loyalty. During the writing of this book, I endured one of the worst upheavals of my personal life, and as a result found powerful irony both in the inability of O.J. Simpson to handle his own emotional vulnerability and the absolute lack of awareness Brian "Kato" Kaelin had when it came to his. I discovered how extraordinarily difficult it is to write about obsession in the third person.

There are several people I wish to thank, all of whom played key roles in the planning and writing of this book. No one deserves greater recognition than Leonard Marks, my good friend for many years and attorney. I believe he is more responsible than anyone for seeing both this project and me through the difficult times. He was constantly reminding me how it was essential to do the right thing.

I wish also to thank my publisher for its support of me.

Mark Lafayette did an incredible amount of work on several of the more tangled legal issues that arose. I thank him and his wife for sacrificing so much time and effort.

There is, as always, my best friend and Chairman of the Board, Dennis Klein. Everyone should be as lucky as I when it comes to friendship.

And to have such good family as I do in the guise of my favorite uncle, Duane.

Mark LaMura and Elizabeth McClellan provided enormous support and vital shelter from the storm with their impenetrable shield of protection.

Steve Fleischman and Dede Allen were also incredibly supportive and helped get me through the long months of anguish, frustration, and exhaustion this project caused.

Sylvie Bordeau proved an able Los Angeles–based personal assistant.

Anne Shames, in Leonard's office, was invaluable, providing support both professionally and personally.

Crystal Zevon is an extraordinary, and extraordinarily beautiful woman. Her sheer presence, as well as her warmth, enthusiasm, discretion, patience, and choice of music during the writing of this book, was invaluable to me.

Also, I want to thank Elizabeth for her loyalty and friendship.

I decline to acknowledge anyone directly involved either with the media that covered and at times smothered this story, including the many reporters and journalists whom I consider my friends, or any of the participants in the case: those who cooperated with me, those who didn't, those who pretended to. To balance all scores and clean all slates, I intend to donate a portion of my proceeds from this book, if any, to Sydney and Justin, the two children of O.J. and Nicole Brown Simpson.

Oh, sea of heartbreak
Lost love and loneliness
Memories of your caress

"SEA OF HEARTBREAK"
performed by Don Gibson
written by Hal David

"It's incredible to see flakes . . . what money can do, how people will sell out. It's just incredible."

— *Brian "Kato" Kaelin,*
From an interview with Marc Eliot,
taped March 4, 1995

Robert Shapiro: Regarding the issue of you getting to have the privilege of staying as Mr. Simpson's guest, it's been pointed out by the prosecutor that that may have had a value of $6,000. It may have had a value greater than that, might it not?

Brian "Kato" Kaelin: Yes.

Robert Shapiro: Regardless of the value, would that be enough to get you to lie in this case, sir?

Brian "Kato" Kaelin: I . . . I will not lie.

Robert Shapiro: For any amount of money?

Brian "Kato" Kaelin: For any amount of money.

Marcia Clark: Mr. Kaelin, you got a lot of money for your appearance on *Current Affair,* didn't you?

Brian "Kato" Kaelin: Yes.

1

*In the Wake of the
Crime of the
Century*

Marcia Clark (Assistant District Attorney): Is that the town house that you were describing that you were going to move into with Nicole?

Brian "Kato" Kaelin: Yes.

Marcia Clark: Now, did you ever move into that town house, sir?

Brian "Kato" Kaelin: No.

Marcia Clark: Why not?

Brian "Kato" Kaelin: I was going to move in and I moved in at O.J.'s.

Marcia Clark: Why not? Why did you do that?

Brian "Kato" Kaelin: Because O.J. asked me to go to his house. I mean, it was part of a deal. . . .

Only God and O.J. Simpson

know if he killed Nicole Brown Simpson and Ron Goldman on the night of June 12, 1994. Nevertheless, or perhaps in spite of truth's maddening elusiveness, speculation surrounding this event has attained world-wide proportions. The murders have been dubbed the Crime of the Century by the media, superseding at least two previous slayings that held that title, the Lindbergh kidnapping/killing and the assassination of President John F. Kennedy.

The so-called Simpson murder case, broadcast live around the globe and starring a world-class celebrity, have transformed the trial into a collective obsession. International TV and radio coverage on a scale usually reserved for major events—the Kennedy Assassination, Watergate, Iran-Contra, the Rodney King trial—or natural disasters, such as floods and earthquakes, has slavishly chronicled every moment of the case and trial.

From the discovery of Nicole Brown Simpson and Ron Goldman's bodies, through O.J.'s "voluntary" return to L.A. the morning of June 13, the infamous slow-speed car chase on a busy Los Angeles freeway, the preliminary hearing, and the actual trial, citizens of the world and Americans in particular have been fixated on the daily events, investing time and attention in the inexorable flow of justice toward a climactic verdict. TV and radio stations covering the trial have experienced the highest ratings in their history. In the eastern part of the United States, where, because of the three-hour time difference, the trial often bleeds into prime time, competing programming has shown significant declines. Every evening, housewives preparing dinner for their families and executives hoisting one at the nearest wood-lined watering hole share a common fascination as they hang on every word of testimony.

What is it about this crime that has so captured the public's imagination? Why have we become obsessed with the fate of an aging, arthritic ex–football player whose life, prior to June 12, had inevitably slipped into cushy meaninglessness to which so many of us think we aspire? Indeed, prior to the murders, O.J. Simpson's life had come to resemble no one's more than Joe DiMaggio's, another of America's once-glorious sports-heroes, the meaningful phase of whose life's work had come to an end at a time when most nonsports careers are still on the ascent. After the glory years, DiMaggio became a huckster for coffee machines. O.J. Simpson ran through airports. Each cashed in as best he could on the glories of his past, that special bottom line where the shadows of age darken youth's fading shine.

Each was obsessed with a beautiful blonde who would ultimately prove unattainable. And each would suffer the humiliation of that loss before the smirks of a once-adoring public.

And each would represent the best their respective minorities had to offer America. As DiMaggio rose to legendary status and entered the pantheon of the Great American Pastime, so did his pride and glory spread throughout the Italian-American community at a time when the country was at war with Mussolini's *Fascista*. DiMaggio's individual triumph became a symbol of every Italian-American's patriotism.

Similarly, O.J. Simpson was a sports hero who, in his era, African-Americans could look to as a role model. His rise to prominence out of the ashes of the Watts riots, the splintering of the civil-rights movement, and amidst increasing racial polarization was a triumph for African-Americans, as well as for a white America seeking a perfect embodiment of its fantasy of how all African-Americans could (i.e., *should*) behave. And because of it, O.J. Simpson was amply rewarded by admittance through the doors that usually keep the peasants out of the American elitist parlor of privilege.

Still, the implications of "the Simpson Case" are not merely skin-deep. They do, in fact, extend to the darkest void that resides between the very cracks of our democratic foundation. Are we not taught from the first grade that crime does not pay? This association between criminal activity and money is retold to us time and again in numerous versions throughout our lives, often with a moral rationale to excuse the more obvious contradictions reality has a way of imposing on abstract beliefs. One only need contrast the mythic pop-culture antics of an Al Capone, whose rise from poverty to great wealth in spite of his murderous ways endeared him to his generation, with our standardized, mythic image of Abraham Lincoln walking that famous mile to return a penny his face would one day emblazon. Corrupt wealth vs. honorable poverty—the great moral dialectic which defines and divides our society.

Still, our social scientists keep insisting that crime is the virus that breeds in the swamp of economic poverty. Those who will remain morally healthy, they warn, are those who can and will work their way up the rungs of that great and revered ladder we call success. Each step up, they say, represents a social order with a corresponding reduction in crime.

This is partially true. It is only the directly violent nature of crime that decreases. A poor man may kill for money to buy food to feed his family. A wealthy man may lead a corporate takeover of food-processing conglomerates that will eliminate enough jobs to send workers into the streets to find new ways to keep feeding their families. The criminal calendars remain filled with the unfortunates at the lower end of the economic scale, far outnumbering those with any degree of wealth. How rare is it for us to catch a glimpse of anyone of social stature appearing in jailhouse jumpsuits, his hands and feet in chains before a judge. And when he does, his fortune allows him the best defense available, make bail, and remain, often for years, among the free.

Rarer still is the criminal suspect both rich *and* famous. Far more often, this class of criminal appears as the embodiment of a middle-class fantasy in movies, TV series, and cheap crime novels, evil bastards endlessly knocking off their wives, children, mistresses, blackmailers, etc. On the occasion when one such seemingly impervious person must actually answer to the court, his or her case is usually defined in terms of the fair "blindness" of the American judicial system. As a result, the public is allowed to hold up these privileged characters in what becomes a freak show of class revenge—the tax-evasion carnival of Leona Helmsley; Darryl Strawberry; and yes, Al Capone; or the family dysfunction House of Horrors of Claus von Bülow accused of trying to murder his wife; Cheryl Crane, Lana Turner's daughter, killing her famous mother's gangster lover; or Patty Hearst captured on videotape robbing a bank.

However, no matter how heinous the crime, punishment for this class remains for the most part nonexistent. Although convicted, von Bülow was eventually found not guilty on retrial and never spent a day behind bars. Helmsley did a few months, Strawberry not a day, Cheryl Crane and Patty Hearst got what amounted to soft slaps on their delicate wrists.

It is, then, one of the great ironies of the Simpson case that, according to our moral canon, the mere *status* of the accused has, in the minds of many (including, perhaps, the defendant himself) eliminated him from, if not being a suspect, then at least having very much to fear from the wrath of the judicial system.

Further, although there is no doubt a core of "anti-Simpsonites" who believe he is guilty of double murder in spite of his social status, there remain an impressive number of observers on both sides of the racial divide (some surveys putting the figure as high as 70 percent) who believe that O.J. Simpson is simply too rich and famous to have committed a violent crime, particularly *this* violent crime. That he must be the victim of some conspiracy. That he must have been a) framed in a drug deal gone bad, b) framed by a white conspiracy to punish him for being too successful an African-American, c) the random victim of a robbery gone horribly wrong, d) exonerated by some other excuse. An amazingly, perhaps alarmingly large percentage of the populace continues to insist the "truth" must be so bizarre, so horribly Hitchcockian in plan and execution, that it has allowed the denial of the fundamentally unexplainable questions of not only how but *why* a man who seemed to have it all—looks, wealth, fame, property, more women than any man could want times ten—would throw it all away in a single moment of mindless vengeance.

One thing seems certain. From everything we now know about O.J. Simpson, up until the night of June 12, his gaze had come to be fixed directly across the ever-widening downstream of his own existential death, from which only a monstrous pair of murders were able to reverse the current of his fate and return him to the shores of the significantly alive. *Whether he did them or not!*

Perhaps that is why we are, as a people, less demanding of the relatively narrow parameters of strictly legal justice than we are in wanting to know why one as gifted and gracious as O.J. Simpson was ultimately unable to fit neatly into the scripted sanity of our accepted social order. Perhaps that is why we seek answers not in the fat legal texts that reside on Judge Ito's great desk of justice, but in the words of the supporting cast of players who have emerged in the wake of the murders.

Unfortunately, most of the "testimony" of these "witnesses" has suffered from large gaps of "lost" information and analytical inaccuracies due at least in part to the questionable bank of their firsthand knowledge, unmanageable bias either for or against O.J., Nicole, or Ron Goldman, or lack of journalistic know-how (if indeed we may still make the distinction between a once sharply delineated borderline that separates so-called legitimate reportage from the tons of tabloid we find ourselves emerged in on a daily basis).

There is, however, one person who holds a unique and therefore privileged position in all of this. His name is Brian "Kato" Kaelin, his profession is actor, or, if you prefer, professional houseboy (or perhaps master opportunist appeals to you), and he actually lived with both victim and accused. While a blood relative of neither, he came to be an intimate of both. Whatever you may think of him, his close proximity to both Nicole and O.J. provided Kaelin with a unique perspective into the private lives of the woman who became a celebrated victim of a tragic murder, the friend who died with her in the alleyway, and the man accused of killing them both.

Kato became Nicole Simpson's tenant in January 1993,

shortly after meeting her on a skiing holiday in Aspen, Colorado. For the next year he lived in her guest house on Gretna Green Way in Brentwood, Los Angeles, during which time he became her friend, her confidant, her father-confessor, her protector, and her soul mate. By the end of his stay, as Nicole was preparing to move to a new house on nearby Bundy Drive, she and her two children had come to regard Kato as one of their own and begged him to keep the brood together. How long did Nicole, Sydney, and Justin want Kato to stay? In Nicole's words, on a note she left for him a few days before the move, "until you find a wife."

What, one wonders, was the relationship between these two that would produce such an extraordinary invitation, not merely to move into a house, but to become, essentially, a member of the family?

Perhaps the answers lie in the days that followed her divorce from O.J. Simpson in the fall of 1992. After what had been more than a decade of violent abuse, Nicole followed through on one of her longtime threats, and divorced her celebrated husband, only to move less than two miles away into a rented space one fifth the size of O.J.'s now famous Rockingham estate. She would later claim she did so for the sake of the kids, to allow them easy access to their father, but a more powerful motive may have been the easy access *she* needed to her former husband.

Apparently, the mutual dependency between Nicole and O.J. kept their emotional battle alive long after the civil war between them had been legally settled, a battle in which she remained psychologically underarmed in the very lair of her violence-prone ex-husband, a man who had physically brutalized her in marriage and continued to loom menacingly in its aftermath. Her instincts, or perhaps her desperation, led her to seek a protector in the person of Kato Kaelin.

11

The symbolic presence of Kato may have been more important to Nicole than his physical being. Here, after all, was a reassuringly young, strong, knight-in-faded-jeans she believed would be willing and able to protect her from the threat of an enraged O.J. Simpson. Indeed, on the night of October 25, 1993, when O.J. came, powerful and threatening like the Big Bad Wolf, and literally tore the back doors off Nicole's house to try to get to her, it was Kato who charged to her rescue, able to blunt the focus and therefore the force of O.J.'s "insane anger" (as Kato described his behavior to me) until the police arrived.

That was the night O.J. Simpson realized that one way or another he would have to remove this last barrier of defense, all that stood between Nicole and his increasingly uncontrollable rage. Less than two months later, as Nicole was preparing to relocate to her new home, it would be without the protective services of Kato Kaelin. Kaelin's excuse for not moving with Nicole? He would later tell me that O.J. appealed to his "sense of decency," saying it was "no longer good for the children to have a man, *any man,* living under the same roof as his ex-wife." O.J. would then provide the "perfect" solution, an irresistible consolation prize. The opportunity to live, rent-free, at Rockingham, where, O.J. told Kato, he would be, as Kato later stated on tape, "treated like King Farouk."

And what did Kato do? Weighing his options, he put the friendship, loyalty, confidence, and trust of Nicole Simpson in one hand, and in the other, the opportunity to move in with the single man she feared most, the man who she had revealed to Kato had a side as monstrous and frightening as one could imagine. Then, with that vacant look of slightly upturned incomprehension many have mistaken for innocence, Kato packed his bags, waved bye-bye to Nicole's fantasy of domestic bliss, and yuk-yukked his way into the bachelor paradise of a man who, in addition to being one of the most attractive and eligible bachelors in Los Angeles, happened to be on the board of no less than a dozen show-business-related corporations. Less than six months later O.J. Simpson would be accused of the murders of Nicole Brown Simpson and Ron Goldman.

Little if any of what Kato witnessed during his year at Nicole's home will likely ever find its way onto the witness stand, falling as it does outside the borders of admissible testimony. Still, his reconstruction for me of that time comes together like the first act of some great and terrible tragedy, at once harrowing, humorous, pathetic, and prophetic.

Had Kato's "O.J. experience" ended after his year at Nicole's, his viewpoint would still hold enormous value. However, when he moved out of the frying pan that was Gretna Green into the burning fire of Rockingham, his perspective was elevated to that wondrous and often unexplainable apex where time and place intersect to produce moments of privilege envied by journalists, dramatists, and storytellers the world over. When, early that January, Kato packed his bags and moved into one of O.J.'s guest houses, one of the great second acts of our day began.

During the five and a half months Kato lived at the football legend's estate, he once again became a human repository, this time for Simpson's innermost feelings about life, about love, and inevitably, about his obsessive desire to reconcile with Nicole. Kato now heard O.J.'s side of the same events he'd first gotten from Nicole's perspective, even as fate guided all three, and Ron Goldman, toward the climactic, murderous events of June 12.

Only God and O.J. Simpson know if he killed Nicole Simpson and Ron Goldman on the night of June 12, 1994. Still, O.J. sits alone in a cell like a modern Richard II, listening

13

to the clock beat of his own heart tick ever louder, facing the grim reality that as once he wasted time so effortlessly, now does time indeed waste him. And so it is we ponder endlessly the so-called facts of his case, and wonder if it was not, after all, the Great Magician's hand of fate that guided Kato Kaelin into the homes and lives of both victim and accused, through the events of the days before the murders and after, and spared his life? As if in some kind of B-movie version of a classic tale, Kato Kaelin washed upon the sandy shore of his own survival and into our consciousness, a postmodern beachboy Ishmael desperate for someone to tell his story.

And that, of course, is when he and I met.

FROM THE TRIAL TESTIMONY OF WITNESS KATO KAELIN— *CALIFORNIA* V. *O.J. SIMPSON*—MARCH 28, 1995:

Marcia Clark: And, as a matter of fact, isn't it true, Mr. Kaelin, that you have a book proposal out for about half a million dollars, right now, don't you?

Kato Kaelin: No.

Marcia Clark: You don't have a book proposal?

Kato Kaelin: No.

Marcia Clark: Don't you have a—aren't you represented by the William Morris Agency to write a book?

Kato Kaelin: No.

Marcia Clark: You're not aware of any contract for half a million dollars that you've been—that you signed?

Kato Kaelin: Oh, I know it's out there, but I haven't done that.

Marcia Clark: You haven't signed it yet.

Kato Kaelin: Oh, no, I heard a story about that. That's not true.

Marcia Clark: You don't have any book proposals out.

Kato Kaelin: No. Don't want to do a book.

Marcia Clark: Plan to write a book in the future, Mr. Kaelin?

Kato Kaelin: As of today, no way.

On March 28, 1995, as Kato Kaelin was denying, under oath, the existence of the book he and I had just spent six months working on together, I was five miles away in my Hollywood apartment, sitting at the desk in my study, working on a new project—or rather, one I had already been deeply involved with and had set aside in November 1994 to collaborate with Kato.

Early in March, nearly three weeks before Kato took the witness stand, I had put the finishing touches on *Star Witness: My Life with Nicole and O.J. Simpson*. Kato had, that same night, given his final approval to the manuscript. I then opened a bottle of expensive red wine to celebrate what had been more than five months of a seven-day-a-week schedule to meet a submission deadline from our publisher of March 15, 1995. We had, in fact, finished nearly two weeks ahead of time, and were eagerly looking forward to getting the book into stores by the first week of April. That night, I believed that nothing and no one could prevent us from going public with what we knew, and taking the so-called trial of the century to a new, significantly higher level of importance.

However, by March 21, the day Kato was sworn in for his formal testimony, I had decided to dissociate myself from the project and him. His increasing equivocation over what he wanted taken out, his criminal and business lawyers' continued interference, and, in my opinion, their attempted manipulation of me had led me to this conclusion.

Things had begun to unravel between Kato and me in the weeks preceding the March 15 submission deadline. Tension had begun to develop between Kato's lawyers and me over the book's content. I had struggled to maintain its integrity, and my own, up until the morning of March 15, when, without informing either my agent or me, Michael Plotkin, Kato's entertainment manager and lawyer, called the publisher to inform them that "we" were not going to deliver the manuscript, now or in the foreseeable future.

My editor—we'll call him Jim—demanded to know why, and was told in the vaguest of terms that there were "problems" with the book's timing. Jim immediately called my agent, who expressed complete and legitimate mystification at Plotkin's actions.

What particularly angered me was that, because of the speed and secrecy of the project, although the publishers had agreed to pay us a six-figure sum, *half upon signing,* the balance upon acceptance and publication, I had not as yet received a penny for my efforts because neither Kato, nor Michael Plotkin, nor I had ever signed the publisher's contract. In fact, I hadn't even seen it, let alone had the opportunity to negotiate terms, because in all the time I had worked on the book, Plotkin hadn't finalized the agreement with the publisher. Not only that, but he had failed to negotiate separately with my agent the terms for my collaborative services. By the time I finished the book *nothing* had as yet been settled, either with the publisher or with me. That was when I decided to end my association with Plotkin and Kato and instructed my agent to halt all further negotiations. I had had enough.

It hadn't always been that way. When I first met Kato, in October 1994 at Michael Plotkin's Century City law offices, he seemed eager to start work. As Kato was to tell me later, he was a fan of both Bruce Springsteen and the book I'd written about him, *Down Thunder Road*, and felt I was a contemporary to which he could "relate."

Still, more than a month went by before I picked up the phone one morning and heard Plotkin's voice on the other end saying it was "time" for all of us to get together. In the intervening weeks, Kato's so-called star had begun to rise. The public reaction to his testimony at the July 1994 preliminary hearings was what one might describe in the O.J. maelstrom as a relatively mild storm off the Catalinas in this the Los Angeles year of Our Lord 19 Ninety and Endless Floods. Kato had caught a wave, no doubt, even if no one could quite describe its size, shape, direction, or force.

Including me. I liked him well enough, found him to be personable, enthusiastic, better looking (less severe) than he came across on camera, and considerably less tense if not altogether goosey; funny in that gag-a-minute fashion failed stand-up comics inevitably seem to carry like a monkey on their backs of their personal lives.

Plotkin, meanwhile, seemed to take a particularly paternalistic pride in having brought Kato and me "together." After we started working, Plotkin's face, an angular structure of enforced looseness that never went anywhere without a briefcase of smiles-for-all-occasions, began to show with increasing regularity what I came to regard as his "unselfconscious," beatific, isn't-Kato-wonderful look, set off with the eerie glow of someone expecting untold future profit.

Kato had, in fact, taken Plotkin on as an entertainment lawyer and Plotkin tried, unsuccessfully it turned out, to get the William Morris Agency to represent his new client. (Reportedly, Plotkin's law partner, "Buddy" Monash, happens to also be partners with O.J. Simpson defense attorney Robert Shapiro in a Los Angeles restaurant, Eclipse.)

Plotkin is one of those Los Angeles lawyers who, by virtue of his practice, became a player in the film business. Upon completion of the preliminary hearings, Plotkin sensed in Kato the potential if not for greatness, at least for big bucks, and offered to take him on, as his agent/lawyer. He then wasted no time trying to convert what amounted to Kato's network-TV debut into a full-time career. After knocking around Hollywood for fifteen years, copping mostly stand-up comedy gigs and a series of go-nowhere jobs on the periphery of the mainstream, at one point trading in his surfer looks to make what amounted to a soft-core porno film, Kato was more than ready to make the leap.

When he and Plotkin approached the West Coast entertainment division of the William Morris agency, it seemed at first quite anxious to sign him, until someone happened to discover the existence of that film. The agency, which has a policy of not representing anyone or anything to do with pornography, decided to pass on him.

One of Plotkin's first brainstorms was to have Kato do a book. He, Plotkin, then did an end run around Beverly Hills and contacted the East Coast literary division of the William Morris Agency, with whom he had a long and successful association, which is how and when my name first came up. Once Kato realized I was the fellow who had done a Springsteen book, after the two meetings I described above, we set about to put down what Kato had been carrying around in his head.

From day one, I had asked for a formal collaboration agreement, a written contract to define our working relationship, financially, legally, etc. Not a problem, Plotkin said. He then decided he should be the one to handle negotiations with publishers. That was fine with me (and my agent), because of the official nonrelationship between Kato and William Morris. In November, Plotkin began talking to several New York publishers, all of whom seemed not only interested, but eager to get their hands on the story. A series of telephone meetings were set up, during one of which Plotkin, Kato, and I talked with various editors.

However, when it came time to ask Kato to describe a few of the incidents he felt would be of most interest to readers, Plotkin would cut him off before he said a word, and inform the publishers they weren't privy to that information.

After several of these meetings, I told Plotkin he was never going to be able sell this book merely on Kato's name, such as it was. His response was that he felt publishers should be throwing money at us, not only because of who Kato was, but because of who *I* was. I admit I smiled at that, welcomed him to the world of publishing, gave him a crash course in "It doesn't happen like that," and told him I thought the only way we could sell this project was for all of us to get

on a plane, fly to New York, sit down with a number of publishers, and have Kato tell them his story. And by the way, have
you done anything at all about a collaboration agreement yet?

Kato couldn't go to New York, Plotkin said, because he was
under subpoena. All right, then, I said, I'll go. However, I'd
need to bring something with me, a proposal with sufficient
information to make the deal. Plotkin asked for a day or two to
think it over, and suggested a meeting later that week.

When I showed up for it, I discovered we had a new problem on our hands. Because one of the preliminary-hearing witnesses had sold his story to *The National Enquirer* for a
reported $15,000, an enraged Gil Garcetti, Los Angeles dis-
trict attorney, had managed to help push through the passage
of a statewide statute, effective January 1, 1995, prohibiting
witnesses from "selling their story" until ninety days after the
end of a trial. Well, I said to Plotkin, that was that.

Not necessarily, he replied. You guys, meaning Kato and me
(he always made an effort to sound like "one of the boys"),
have already started. We're therefore exempt, he insisted,
according to the statute's built-in grace period. And yes, we
ought to go ahead and do some kind of formal proposal.

Kato and I then set a time to meet. He suggested we go that
night to a party at Bar One, in Beverly Hills, where "all the
models hang." He thought it would be a good place for us to
plan the proposal. I thought it might be a good idea to see him
in his element.

I met Kato at the club that evening and witnessed firsthand
the kind of fun craziness he seemed to naturally attract—gorgeous actresses and models making fools out of themselves for
the possibility of I'm still not sure what.

It was now December, and in spite of a bad case of the flu,
I arranged for Kato to come over to my place in Hollywood,
and sit for a ninety-minute interview. I planned to use that tape

and an accompanying summary as the major portion of my presentation.

That interview took place on December 27, 1994. In January, I flew to New York to begin a series of meetings. Knowing the kind of material I had, I was not surprised at the size and number of contracts Plotkin was offered. To all of them, he said thank you very much, and informed me it was time to come back to Los Angeles and start writing.

Halfway though the book and still without any collaboration agreement, it occurred to me that there was nothing to prevent Kato (and Plotkin) from cutting me out of the deal. I was told by my agent to stop being paranoid, that there was a deadline looming and I should "keep writing."

And so I did. For the next two months Kato and I virtually lived together at my place. He would arrive early each morning, head straight for the kitchen telephone and immediately start to return all his calls, local and long distance, while loading up on caffeine. We would then shoot the shit about the night before and set our social calendar for the one coming up. Usually, after about an hour, he would feel comfortable enough to settle into my big black leather easy chair and attach a microphone to his shirt collar. I'd take the seat opposite and begin that day's interview.

Over the months Kato proved an extraordinary subject. Early on, it had become apparent that he had a great still-untold story (one he had certainly given neither to the grand jury nor at the preliminary hearing), and perhaps more intriguing to me, seemed increasingly desperate to tell it.

That was fine with me, as long as certain rules were followed. As I do with everyone I interview, I insisted that our discussions be held in total privacy—no third parties present, no friends, no agents, no associates (especially lawyers)—and that the tapes not be copied. I was to be the only one who had them. That was and is the best method I know of to ensure confidentiality.

I realized from the start that the best approach to Kato was not from a legalistic posture, not to cross-examine him, but to simply talk as if I were one of the millions of curious electronic onlookers eager to know what he knew. Fortunately, I was the one person out of those millions who now had the opportunity to sit with him face-to-face. And expect answers.

We began our conversations with the events of June 11, 1994, the day before the murders. From there we zigzagged through time and memory, backward, forward, at times sideways, associatively lurching from Kato's Midwest upbringing to his upcoming testimony at the trial. We covered those events that everyone knew about, and those no one knew of. We talked in depth about the year Kato lived with Nicole at Gretna Green, and his nearly six months at O.J.'s Rockingham estate. Every time I thought I had heard it all, new stories would emerge, tales that sometimes made me laugh, and other times caused my body temperature to drop several degrees.

Certain days he seemed to want to do his thing at hyperspeed. Other days his words would slow to a crawl as he'd look away and appear to be lost in the prison of his own uneasiness.

And there were times he seemed so distracted as to be unable to get into anything, usually caused by an upcoming date with a woman he particularly liked, whom he would constantly talk about. Those days he would wind up being simply no good to me at all.

The woman thing with him was a constant source of fascination. Some of it, naturally, was fun. Like hanging out at *Playboy*'s L.A. offices, or at the clubs along Sunset where women are as curvaceous, plentiful, and alike as those three-ring pretzels all the bars serve with drinks.

I've been known in my day to make a complete idiot out of myself when pursuing women. I've even known some fellows who are actually good at it. However, I have never met anyone like Kato. He could score with women as if he were the living antidote every beautiful young "thing" needed to prevent herself from immediately turning into an ugly old hag.

We'd often double, usually me paired with his date's roommate (no model or actress type lives alone in L.A.), during which time I'd have the opportunity to observe Kato at his most incomprehensible. For instance, one night on the way to pick up our dates for the evening, he turned to me and said, "Marc, I don't know what I'm going to do. I can't go to the grocery store without being recognized! People are waiting for me outside my apartment! I don't have any more privacy!" With his next breath he suggested we have dinner with the women at Chaya, one of the hippest, busiest places-to-be-seen in Beverly Hills.

One morning after one of those nights I asked Kato if he ever wanted to actually have a relationship with any of these women and he looked at me like I was crazy. "Not until I'm fifty," he said, making fifty sound like ninety, adding "Been there, done that. Have a kid. Don't want another."

More than once, when it came time to pay the check for dinner, Kato would then turn to me and ask if I could put it on my credit card until we got back to his place, where he would "settle up." A reconciling for which I still await. Another lesson in the Kato Way of Life.

So it was that we lurched toward a conclusion of sorts and our approaching March 15 deadline. Plotkin had apparently agreed to that date with the publisher early on, when he still believed Kato would complete his testimony in January. As for that

California statute, the publisher had no fear of it, and was willing to take it on. We all believed we could get it overturned (as a similar statute had been in New York, the so-called Son-of Sam law). Besides, the publisher felt, a good old-fashioned public legal slugfest would probably sell a lot of books.

What Plotkin or anyone else apparently didn't count on was the series of increasingly bizarre delays that wreaked havoc on the court calendar, highlighted by the two-week interruption of the trial caused by the Rosa Lopez debacle. Lopez, the housekeeper of one of O.J.'s neighbors, had claimed she saw his White Bronco parked outside the Rockingham estate at a time that would have made it impossible for him to have committed the murders. The defense had rubbed their palms together at the thought of her testimony, until she suddenly announced she was leaving the country. At that point Cochran and company were able to convince Judge Ito to halt the prosecution's case, have Lopez testify for the defense without a jury present, videotape it, and decide later whether or not to use it.

During this unbelievable turn, the prosecution announced that it was rescheduling its next series of witnesses. Kato had originally been set to follow Lopez. Now Marcia Clark intended to call Detectives Lang, Vannatter, Phillips, and Fuhrman. As a result, Kato was pushed back first into February, and eventually to March.

By the time I finished writing the book, he still hadn't testified. I had worked on one of those night and day continuums, taping sessions with Kato during the day, running around with him at night, and every second in between holed up in my study, often taking a portable computer to bed with me to work through the night and next day.

Still, there were two problems confronting Kato and his team. The first was that he was going to be called *after* the book was submitted. Although one of the key prosecution witnesses, this would make him vulnerable to the defense, who could then accuse him of "cashing in." Should that happen, the district attorney's office might then come after Kato for having violated the statute. This action seemed far more likely if the book damaged his value to the state's case.

The second was that Kato had never signed anything in relation to the book. I knew from the publisher that a contract had been sent to Plotkin that might very well still be sitting on his desk right alongside the unsigned and unnegotiated collaboration deal between Kato and me. With the deadline for submission approaching, the publisher became understandably quite nervous. As did I. They wouldn't release any of the signing money until they had a valid contract. Plotkin apparently did not want Kato to sign the contract until he testified.

Further, Plotkin now wanted the manuscript gone over by Kato's criminal lawyer, William Genego. That disturbed me. I had no problems with Kato's people wanting to go over the material; just with their timing. It was the day before we were about to hand in a book, still with no signed contract or collaboration agreement, and now suddenly, at the last possible moment, Kato's people informed me they wanted to "go over" certain parts of the book they felt didn't work in his best interests.

Frankly, I didn't get it. After all, I had already been through a series of what I considered friendly skirmishes with Kato during the writing period. As the world would learn when he testified, Kato Kaelin is one of the great equivocators. It became clear to me that, although he had told me everything on tape, when he saw his own words in print he was often horrified at what he had said. "We have to change this," or "we have to eliminate this," or "O.J. is going to be angry at me if I say this," or "don't you think the family [the Browns] will hate me if I say that" became a part of an ever-increasing litany of fear and calculation on Kato's part. Certainly the fear was understandable. He had told me things no one else knew. In spite of his empty-headed beach-bum manner, he was an excellent observer of people and events, one of the reasons he was always so successful in pulling off his so-called house-guest persona. When it comes time to taking advantage of a situation, Kato is second to none. That's a type of behavior that is almost always accompanied by a fair amount of fear. The skill comes in juggling a lot of potentially explosive bombs. The fear comes when you think about dropping one. It slowly dawned on Kato that this time he might have dropped them all. At least a dozen times during our meetings Kato would sit back, look at me, and ask if I thought O.J. might be angry at him for saying certain things. I'd ask why. He'd say because it might hurt O.J. I'd ask if Kato was willing to lie to prevent O.J. from feeling hurt. No, he'd say, that wasn't it. What if O.J. were acquitted, and held a grudge.

So?

So, he'd reply, as if this were something he'd thought about for quite some time, what if O.J. comes after me? In the end, fear is always about self-preservation, and it was quite clear to me that Kato had begun to fear for his life.

His solution was a simple one. To him. All we had to do was change a few things, a little verbal surgery to ensure that nobody got hurt.

Nobody got hurt? What about Nicole and Ron Goldman? I reminded him. Did he think their lives deserved the truth? That question usually bent Kato over, to a point where he'd hold his stomach and rock back and forth with indecision.

In the end, he found a solution of sorts to his moral dilemma by simply passing the hot potato along to Plotkin, who in turn handed it to Genego.

The day the book was to have been submitted, after Plotkin

made his call to the publisher, Jim, our editor, called my agent, who in turn called Plotkin to find out what was going on. Plotkin told him all he wanted was a couple of extra days so that Genego could give the book the go-ahead. By the end of the week, he assured us, it would be submitted. My agent called Jim, who, although angry, agreed to the extension.

The next day Jim called my agent to tell him that because of the delay, the publisher now wanted to see the manuscript before issuing any money for it. That, of course, was completely unacceptable to me. The original deal had been half the advance delivered on signing. Because Plotkin had not signed the contract and had failed to deliver on time, the publishing house, perhaps figuring it was being squeezed for more money, seized the opportunity and tried to outmaneuver him. It didn't seem to bother anyone that I was caught in the middle, hadn't gotten paid, and was watching two lawyers and my so-called collaborator going at the book with a set of hot shears like it was a field overgrown with weeds.

I called Plotkin myself the next morning, and was told once again that it was only a matter of a day or two before Genego would have his changes. Holding my anger in check, I decided to wait and see how bad they were, and if I could find some way to live with them.

By the end of the week, having heard nothing from anybody except Jim, who called again, this time to ask if I might unofficially slip him the manuscript so he could look at the material and maybe start the editorial process—an idea I was less than thrilled with and refused to agree to—I decided to call Genego myself. I thought perhaps by speaking with him directly, I might be able not only to speed things up but to convince him to let certain things in the book stand.

I called Genego on Monday, March 20, and was told he was "too busy at the moment to come to the phone." That call was followed by yet another, to my agent, during which I instructed him to hold no further meetings with Plotkin regarding any contracts or agreements for my book or services. I had finally come to the realization that the deal was unworkable. My agent's reaction was that, in fact, no meetings or negotiations were currently happening, he was completely in the dark as to the motives of Plotkin and company, and deeply sorry that the situation had deteriorated to this point.

The next day Genego called to say he was not going to discuss the book, that Kato was his client, and it was not in his, Genego's, best interests to have any further communication with me.

I planned to tell Genego that although I had originally intended this call to be about finding out if he had made his changes, I had decided instead to withdraw my services. Before I got that far, however, he informed me that *a week earlier* he had recommended to Plotkin and Kato that this book should never see the light of day. When I asked why, he refused to comment except to say there were too many "things" in it that might compromise the integrity of his client when he took the witness stand.

I was furious. No one from Plotkin's or Genego's office had bothered to contact me about anything since the previous week. Kato, who had been in Las Vegas during all of this, called me that Saturday night from his hotel, where he was registered under an assumed name, presumably because he'd left the state without the permission of the district attorney's office.

According to Kato, he had decided to go to Las Vegas anyway to film a small part he'd landed in a TV show, with the understanding on the producer's part that should he have to return to L.A., they would shoot around him.

I told Kato how angry and upset I was at the actions of his lawyers. He acted surprised, and said he hadn't heard anything from either Plotkin or Genego, and that as far as he was concerned, everything was fine. He said he was looking forward to the book's publication, and making a lot of money.

He then said he had thought about asking if he could sleep on my sofa during the time he'd be testifying, because he was afraid of being constantly hounded by the press if he went home. I told him he was, of course, welcome at anytime, but that it probably wasn't a good idea for us to be seen together. If the press were following him around, as he claimed, how long, I asked, did he think it would take for them to figure out what we were doing?

He laughed, said something about how I was always looking in every direction at the same time, told me he'd "had" two of his costars, one was "in love" with him, and he wanted to fix me up with a friend of a friend when he got back to L.A., a woman who worked at Warner Bros. he described as "the brainy type, the way you like them." I told him how much I appreciated his watching out for my interests, and hung up, convinced he was lying. Whenever he'd been with me, he'd clock in with Plotkin every hour or so. Surely by now, Kato had to know that the deal for the book was, in fact, dead.

On Tuesday, March 21, Detective Philip Vannatter, one of the first officers to arrive at the murder scene, completed his testimony, which had begun the previous week, and after a relatively brief recall of Detective Lange, one of Vannatter's partners in the investigation, Kato was finally set to testify.

I was at my desk in my home office, working on the book I had set aside in order to work on Kato's, watching with one eye his testimony on a small TV set next to my computer. Although I no longer considered myself a part of the project, I was still curious to see how he handled himself on the witness stand. I also fully expected him to tell the court what he had already told me, with, if anything, some elaboration in areas he had been reluctant to discuss during our sessions.

What I heard instead was one of the most astonishing displays of cowardice—I have no other word for it—that I have ever experienced. It began early on with a twitching, jerky Kato trying to slide through on his good humor (*Clark:* You feel a bit nervous today? *Kato:* Feel great!) until he was confronted with the first significant question. Marcia Clark asked him how he met Nicole, and he replied that he and his friend Grant Cramer had decided to go to Aspen for the 1992 Christmas holidays. When Clark pressed Kato to tell the court who else he met that week, besides Nicole, I and the rest of the world received our first public dose of Kato's special brand of selective memory:

> **Marcia Clark:** Did you all [Grant, Nicole, Faye Resnick, Kato] spend that whole week together?
>
> **Brian "Kato" Kaelin:** I—quite a few people. But basically, it was myself, Grant Cramer, Faye Resnick was there, and Nicole and other people that I—the names I can't think of 'em right now, but other people.

I stopped writing, sat back, put my foot up, rested an elbow on my knee, dropped my jaw to my palm and wondered how Kato could have "forgotten" about Jerry Ginsburg, in whose condo Kato had told me Nicole stayed for the entire trip, and whom O.J. hated and would later refer to as a "pimp"—either forgotten or had decided to omit from his testimony.

On the circumstances surrounding his move from Nicole's house to O.J.'s, the following transpired:

Marcia Clark: Did he indicate anything to you with respect to what he thought of the fact that you'd been living in the same house as Nicole Brown?

Brian "Kato" Kaelin: Well, they were trying to work things out and I said that I understood. It wasn't—I thought maybe I shouldn't be a guy in the house and I would go there, kind of like that.

Marcia Clark: Did he indicate to you in some way that he thought it inappropriate for you to be in the same house with her, or he didn't like it?

Brian "Kato" Kaelin: Not . . . didn't like it, but it probably wouldn't be right.

Marcia Clark: And why wouldn't it be right?

Brian "Kato" Kaelin: I don't know the answer.

And how, I wondered, could he have forgotten what he had told me about that day? That O.J. had told him he didn't think "it was right for you to be living under the same roof as Nicole and the kids," and that he, Kato, had replied, "I totally understand." Or that Nicole's outraged response was to tell Kato that he was being "manipulated" by O.J.

By the end of his first day of testimony, it had become clear to me that Kato, whether on his own or under advice from others, had decided to neutralize his testimony as much as possible. The portrait of O.J. that began to emerge was a surprisingly benign one, a picture of a "great guy," one of the boys, someone who wasn't particularly interested in seeing Nicole again, who loved to play golf, watch basketball, and dutifully fly off to promote rental cars. According to Kato's trial version, O.J. was a valiant prince of light rather than a malevolent creature of the dark.

As for the details of the day of the murder, and what had been suggested by the prosecution—that O.J. Simpson had reached a point of rage that led him to kill, and that Kato would be the one to verify this rage, as well as solidify the time line of opportunity—Kato's testimony had thus far provided little, if any, help.

Kato's second day of testimony began with his description of the Rockingham estate the day of the murders, and then shifted to O.J.'s relationship with Paula Barbieri, his current girlfriend. When Clark asked Kato about O.J.'s feelings for Paula, it was to establish motive by showing that O.J. hadn't, in fact, "moved on" with his life at all but was desperately, if hopelessly, still in love with Nicole.

Marcia Clark: And what did [O.J.] tell you about Paula?

Brian "Kato" Kaelin: [after a series of objections from the defense, overruled by Judge Ito] From what I remember, that she wanted to go, and I believe O.J. didn't want her to go.

Marcia Clark: So he didn't want her to go to the recital with him?

Brian "Kato" Kaelin: At that time?

Marcia Clark: Uh-hum.

Brian "Kato" Kaelin: Yes.

Marcia Clark: Did he tell you what his feeling were about Paula?

Brian "Kato" Kaelin: [after a series of objections by the defense, overruled by Judge Ito] That he wasn't sure as far as just the one—maybe the one, maybe not the one.

Marcia Clark: I'm sorry?

Brian "Kato" Kaelin: To spend—you know, to be the one to be with? Like for life?

Marcia Clark: Okay. He wasn't sure if she was the one for him? [after a series of defense objections, sustained by Judge Ito, the question is rephrased]. Can you please tell us what did the defendant say to you about his feelings for Paula?

Brian "Kato" Kaelin: Not being sure if Paula was going to be the one to be with . . . it was undecided.

What he told me was substantially different. According to Kato, Paula was, to O.J., little more than a great sexual partner, someone who could arouse him like no other woman, but that marriage, and children, which she wanted and he absolutely didn't, was out of the question.

Still, none of this seemed substantial enough for strong

concern, until Marcia Clark began to zero in on the day of the murder. Kato's account of what happened in the hours immediately preceding and the days that followed were filled with odd variations, conspicuous omissions, and at the same time even more stunning details he somehow "forgot" to tell Marcia Clark under direct examination. The actions and character of O.J. Simpson seemed to be completely different from what he had told me, and, it appeared, Marcia Clark knew it. Time and again she would press for some clarification, or a bit of information she apparently expected but didn't get from Kato.

As he continued to sweat it out on the witness stand, using the occasional joke to try to both lighten the pressure of the moment and endear himself to his "audience," I finally began to understand what he had been telling me all these months. He had indeed been genuinely caught off guard at the preliminary hearing, he admitted, and hadn't expected the kind of immediate, positive reaction to what he once referred to in jest over a cup of coffee as his "performance," but, having found a "vehicle," he was going to "maximize this opportunity to the fullest."

It had been a strange choice of words, and made me stop and think about just who this fellow was. *Opportunity?* Is that how he saw all of it? When I asked him, he did what has become a well-known gesture of his to trial goers. He smirk-smiled, bent his elbows, put his palms up, and shook his head. "I'm an actor," he said. "Shouldn't I be allowed to pursue my career? I'm going to go for it now that I've got an opening. I'm going to make a career for myself that's going to last longer than fifteen minutes. Wait and see."

It was the following exchange that finally sent Marcia Clark into the quiet fury that led to her declaring Kato a hostile witness. I watched my TV, fascinated, as this exchange—

regarding O.J. Simpson's behavior following the Sunday afternoon recital featuring his daughter Sydney—took place:

FROM THE TRIAL TESTIMONY OF BRIAN "KATO" KAELIN—
CALIFORNIA *y. O.J. SIMPSON*—MARCH 27, 1995
(Direct examination):

Marcia Clark: Was the defendant upset when he spoke
of trying to see Sydney at the recital?

Brian "Kato" Kaelin: There was some upsetness [sic],
yes.

Marcia Clark: Did that upsetness increase at some
point during his conversation with you after the
recital?

Brian "Kato" Kaelin: No.

Marcia Clark: Never increased?

Brian "Kato" Kaelin: The—upsetness after the recital,
talking about it? No.

Marcia Clark: Was there any other remark he made
about the events of the recital in which he seemed
more agitated or upset than when he spoke about
trying to see Sydney?

Brian "Kato" Kaelin: About the dresses?

Marcia Clark: Yes.

Brian "Kato" Kaelin: Yes, he said that about the—wearing dresses when they're grandmothers?

Marcia Clark: Yes.

Brian "Kato" Kaelin: Yes. There was—but the upset—there was upsetness, but it was more upset about the statement of Sydney, but both—but more with Sydney not being—able to see him.

Marcia Clark: Is that the way you want to leave it, Mr. Kaelin? Is that right? He was more upset talking about Sydney than he was talking about Nicole? Is that your testimony?

Brian "Kato" Kaelin: That—yes.

Clark continued to press Kato on this point, citing how, during his preliminary testimony, he had "forgotten" the details of his conversation with O.J. and, apparently, the reality of his mood. She quoted his earlier testimony, in which he had said that O.J.'s demeanor during Sydney's performance was "non-chalant. It was relaxed."

Marcia Clark: And now you're testifying today, sir, that he was upset when he talked about Sydney.

Brian "Kato" Kaelin: At the time, that's what I remember.

Marcia Clark: But you didn't remember that back on June twentieth of 1994, is that right?

Brian "Kato" Kaelin: Yes.

Marcia Clark: And now you remember that?

Brian "Kato" Kaelin: Yes.

Marcia Clark: And what about during the time that she made—that he made the remark about Nicole wearing tight dresses? Was he upset when he said that?

Brian "Kato" Kaelin: More upset with the Sydney statement, but maybe just a bit with that, with the—

Marcia Clark: Just a bit? I'm sorry?

Brian "Kato" Kaelin: Yes. Can you show me [in the preliminary hearing transcript]—

At this point, Clark was genuinely shocked at the sheer incomprehensibility of Kato's responses. Here was her supposed key witness not only changing his testimony, but seeming to reinvent his memories of the day of the murders *on the spot.* After a brief exchange with Judge Ito, she continued:

Marcia Clark: So your testimony now is that he was upset about the Sydney incident, but just a bit upset about Nicole, her tight dresses, is that right?

Brian "Kato" Kaelin: Ummmm . . .

Marcia Clark: Is that what you testified?

Brian "Kato" Kaelin: Yes, that's—yes.

Marcia Clark: [after reading back Kato's preliminary testimony hearing when he described O.J. that day as having been extremely upset] Do you recall giving that testimony, sir?

Brian "Kato" Kaelin: Yes.

Marcia Clark: You didn't say there he was "a little bit upset," did you?

Brian "Kato" Kaelin: Ummm, no.

Marcia Clark: You're changing your testimony now, Mr. Kaelin?

Brian "Kato" Kaelin: No.

Marcia Clark: Was he upset or wasn't he, when he talked about Nicole and her tight dresses?

Brian "Kato" Kaelin: No, not real upset.

That was enough for Clark. She turned to the judge and made what many consider an extraordinary, open-court pronouncement:

Kato Kaelin: The Whole Truth

Marcia Clark: Your honor, I'm going to ask leave of
the court to take this witness as a hostile witness.

Was I surprised at her actions? Not at all. I had watched Kato
fandango his way through six days of testimony, with Marcia Clark
all the while trying to focus his responses. Everyone had expected
Kato to coffin-nail O.J.'s defense. Instead, it became quite clear to
me that the only constant in Kato's mind was the direction of his
career. Here, once again, he had, as you'll see, omitted a vital
piece of information that altered the meaning of his testimony.

Word flew among the press that he was scared, that he had
been reached, that he had decided he couldn't "rat" on his
friend. All of which may have had some degree of truth.
However, I felt certain that the reason he had chosen to back
off was simply a career move. Brian "Kato" Kaelin didn't want
to be known as the guy who convicted his generous, selfless,
good-time pal, O.J. Simpson.

Once Judge Ito granted Clark the right to consider Kato a
hostile witness, she continued to grill him, now shifting her
focus from accreditation to discreditation; from the piecing
together of evidentiary information to characterizing his contradictions. Amazingly, the prosecution's key witness seemed
to have become one of the defense's best weapons.

This was followed by a relatively brief cross-examination by
O.J. defense attorney Robert Shapiro, who appeared more the
loving, protective uncle than the hard-nosed interrogator.
Shapiro asked Kato the following:

Robert Shapiro: Mr. Kaelin, has anyone from any
tabloids approached you to sell your story?

Brian "Kato" Kaelin: Yes.

Robert Shapiro: Who has approached you?

Brian "Kato" Kaelin: Everyone. Every tabloid.

Robert Shapiro: How much money have you been offered?

Brian "Kato" Kaelin: Close to a million, I guess.

Robert Shapiro: Have you accepted any money from any tabloids for your story?

Brian "Kato" Kaelin: No.

After a few more questions, Marcia Clark redirected, and that's when Kato said there was no proposal out, no signed book contract, and went on to state that "No. Don't want to do a book . . . as of today, no way." Kato had successfully gotten out of a tight spot, with the unwitting help of Marcia Clark's rather obtuse questioning.

I stared at the TV in disbelief. Sitting next to my computer was a completed copy of the manuscript and, next to it, nearly seventeen hours of taped interviews we had done.

Not more than ten minutes went by before the phone began to ring. Everyone in my close professional circle began to call, to find out what was going on. The phone continued to ring for nearly two hours, until finally I had to disconnect it. Then the fax machine took over.

I began to wonder, had I somehow been set up? Had Kato and his attorneys tried to feed me information that would, if released, do Kato's job for him, only with my name on it? And what if I sat on the tapes, and Marcia Clark, who apparently knew that we had done a book, and the players involved, suddenly sent a team of marshals to get them . . . could I be accused of being an accessory after the fact?

As a journalist and biographer who has tackled some fairly controversial subjects in the past, including the previously unknown connection between Walt Disney and the FBI, one of my strengths has always been, as it is with every investigative journalist, my sources. If I volunteered these tapes, I feared my career might very well come to an end. It didn't take long to construct an additional number of nightmare scenarios. For instance, what if Kato suddenly claimed that I had come to him, instead of the other way around, and suggested we make up some wild stories about O.J., with the promise of making— pardon the expression—a killing.

I knew I had to do something. I decided to call Leonard Marks, in New York City, an attorney I had known for many years on both a professional and personal level. Prior to going into private practice, Marks had been a federal prosecutor, a federal prosecution consultant on the Watergate case, and his previous clients had included the Beatles, Eddie Murphy, and Billy Joel; he was the one person I felt could help in a situation that was beginning to cling to me like cold sweat.

When I told Leonard what was going on, he recommended that we contact the district attorney's office immediately. He pointed out something that I have never since lost sight of: this was no longer about a book, this was about murder. If I had information that could help the prosecution, I really had no choice but the morally correct one. I had to tell them what I knew.

I asked Leonard to give me a day to think about everything.

I hoped during that time to hear from either Kato or Plotkin, with some explanation that would make any sense at all. When, after a day went by with, it seemed, phone calls from everyone I knew and hundreds of reporters I didn't, I called Leonard back and told him I was prepared at least to talk to Marcia Clark and confirm the existence of the book.

Leonard told me not to go anywhere for the next hour. From his Manhattan office, he called Marcia Clark and Chris Darden, who were on a lunch break from the trial and awaiting our call. After introductions were made, Clark began her informal discussion with the one question I hoped I wouldn't have to answer. "Mr. Eliot," she said, "when you were working on the book with Kato, did you make any tape recordings?"

I paused, took a long beat, and said, "Yes, I did."

"I want them."

"No," Leonard said. "Not without a subpoena."

"If that's the way we have to go, then we will."

Leonard then said he would work out the details with her, and that in the meantime, while she had me on the phone, she could continue to question me.

She wanted to know about the day of the murders. In particular, if Kato said anything about O.J.'s mood, and what, if anything, he had left out of his testimony. She was looking for evidence that would prove motive.

There was plenty. For instance, when Kato told me about O.J.'s return from his daughter's dance recital, in addition to the business about the black dresses and the grandmothers—"were they going to dress like that when they were grandmothers?"—according to Kato, O.J. had also said that he thought Nicole was dressed to go clubbing that night. There was a silence on the phone, because all four of us knew what that implied. It spoke directly to motive, to O.J.'s relentless possessiveness and jealousy concerning Nicole's sexual life after their divorce.

We talked for at least another forty minutes, with me answering questions about what Kato had told me, on tape, and with Marcia Clark and Chris Darden becoming increasingly friendly and openly appreciative of what we were doing. When they suggested that they might want to talk with me further, Leonard informed them that he would be present for any discussions, and if necessary, he would get on a plane and fly to L.A. to do so. "You'd love it here," Darden said to him. "The weather's really beautiful. Come on out."

The phone call ended with Clark and Darden having to rush back for their afternoon courtroom session. Leonard immediately called me back and told me to start copying those tapes. He instructed me to make three copies—one for him, one for the DA, and one for me, and when I was finished, to put the originals in a vault.

For the next day and a half I worked around the clock, laboriously copying each of the seventeen tapes on my double-cassette-deck/cd unit, not wanting to risk taking them to a professional copying house. When I finished, I called Leonard and told him I was shipping him his copy. He got them the next day and, after listening to several, called me. I could tell from the tone of his voice that he was more than a little concerned.

"Do you have any idea what is on these tapes?" he asked.

"I believe I do," I said.

"We have got to get these to the prosecution. This is going to change the entire case. I can't believe they haven't been able to get this Kato character to tell them what he told you."

"I know," I said, growing increasingly depressed at the position I was finding myself in.

"Kato will probably deny the veracity of what he said to you," Leonard concluded. "But there's no denying the way those interviews were conducted. He had no idea what you were going to ask him, did he?"

"No."

"He didn't have notes, did he?"

"No."

"And the more time he spent with you, the more he opened up, is that right?"

"That's exactly right. It was as though he needed to tell someone what he knew, and I guess I was that person. And look where it's gotten me."

"Don't worry. Just tell the truth."

"What if they call me to testify?" It wasn't an empty question. Marcia Clark and Chris Darden had made it clear that they were going to include that possibility in the subpoenas, in effect putting me on the same forty-eight-hour notice on which they had Kato. Leonard had dealt with them for quite some time on this point, and also on whether or not I was going to give them a copy of the manuscript. I didn't want to do that. After a long give-and-take, the prosecutors agreed that the manuscript was less important than the tapes, especially after I explained to them how Kato and his attorneys had kept wanting to edit the manuscript.

The next day, Gary Schram, a lieutenant in the Los Angeles District Attorney's Bureau of Investigation, came by to personally deliver a copy of the subpoena to me (after Leonard had been "officially" served in New York) and took several of the tapes.

A total of three subpoenas were served. The DA wanted the tapes, the original book proposal, and a copy of the unsigned contract with the publisher. Each time a subpoena was served, Lieutenant Schram would come by to pick up the material. On his last visit, the lieutenant, a tough, strong, no-nonsense sort of fellow with a surprisingly easy smile, put a hand on my shoulder and personally thanked me "for doing the right thing." He also happened to mention William Hodgman, the deputy district attorney originally in charge of the prosecution until he took ill and moved to the background. Hodgman was a Bruce Springsteen fan, and, when the trial was over, would love to have an autographed copy of my book. *Wait a minute, I thought to myself, Wasn't this how I got involved in the whole mess in the first place?*

I told Schram I happened to have an extra copy I wouldn't mind giving to Hodgman. Schram asked me to sign it, and then insisted on paying for it. I don't usually charge people for gifts, but in this instance I figured it was unquestionably the right thing to do.

I walked the lieutenant to his car. Just before he got in, he turned to me and asked if I thought I was in any danger. I told him no. He asked if I had gotten any unusual calls, or seen anybody I didn't know lurking near my home. I then informed him of the death threat I had received one night while I was working on Kato's book. It was about ten o'clock. I was alone editing the manuscript when the phone rang. I picked it up, and a deep, male voice on the other end said that if this book came out, the next time my name appeared in print would be at the top of the obituary pages. Not a pleasant experience.

Schram gave me a card with a special twenty-four-hour phone number. "If you have any problems, if you think anything at all seems suspicious, I want you to call me. I am available at any time, and I can have someone out here in less than two minutes." I thanked him, we shook hands, and I watched him drive off.

For the next several days I remained in constant touch with Leonard, who assiduously worked his way through the tapes. Each evening we would go over their contents. Leonard seemed more amazed with each tape, about what Kato said about O.J., what he said about Nicole, and the emerging picture of the ongoing psychological warfare that had really existed between the two.

Clark and Darden spent the weekend of April 1 and 2 going over the tapes and concluded that there was enough legitimate information to submit them as evidence to the court. That Monday, April 3, they handed them over to Judge Ito, under seal. The purpose was similar to the defense's during the preliminary hearings when it had submitted the envelope of "unknown" content. The tapes were made available to Judge Ito to listen to and decide if they would be admissable as evidence. In mid-April the tapes were unsealed and handed over to the defense under the rules of discovery.

In the meantime Leonard suggested I leave Los Angeles for a while and come to New York. He felt it was no longer completely safe for me to be in L.A., and that once the tapes were revealed, I would be deluged by the press, and perhaps the court, both prosecution and defense. I was undecided about uprooting my existence until I received a most unexpected call from, of all people, Michael Plotkin.

His voice was the epitome of sunshine as he began one of his long, pseudo-philosophical (and one-way) discussions with me about Kato's "magical effect" on the imagination of America. "What was it," he asked with the same kind of simplistic whimsy one finds on children's playroom wallpaper, "that America loves about Kato?"

I had no answer.

Without ever mentioning Kato's testimony, Plotkin said I should come into his office for a meeting. "You know," he said, "Kato's hotter than ever. I think we can put together a movie development deal that should really make us some big money. Kato, of course, wants you in on it."

"You know," I said, "I could go broke making deals with you guys." Plotkin laughed, and said I should come in that Thursday, late in the afternoon, to "straighten everything out."

I had no idea what he meant by that. I called Leonard to tell him about the phone call and he said that under no circumstances should I meet with Plotkin, or Kato, and that I should get on a plane *now*. I knew he was right. Besides, he wasn't the only one urging me to go to New York. For personal reasons having nothing at all to do with the O.J. Simpson case, I had been planning to head back east anyway. The next morning, just before I left for the airport, I called Plotkin back; his opening comment to me was how awful it was that on such a beautiful Los Angeles day (it was about eighty degrees) he had to be "locked up" in his office. I told him I felt very sorry for him and that, by the way, I had to cancel our meeting because I was going to New York.

Plotkin seemed genuinely thrown, and asked if I couldn't come even for a few minutes before I left town. I told him that I just didn't feel right about making any more "deals" with him and Kato, and that I had a career to concentrate on that they had effectively stalled for the better part of the past six months. Plotkin told me to be sure and call him "the second" I returned to L.A.

My first night in New York, I watched Kato on a Barbara Walters special, a spot originally intended to launch our book. There he was, all smiley and long-haired, acting as if he'd just come from being nominated for an Academy Award, without the slightest trace of sadness for the reality of the situation that had brought him to the spotlight in the first place. That night I found him particularly arrogant, insensitive, self-centered, self-promoting, and altogether distasteful. I asked myself, perhaps several months too late, who the hell was this guy, anyway?

That first week in New York I met daily with Leonard, going over the tapes, trying to decide on my next move. Then, on Monday, April 17, the transcript of a sidebar conference was released; the conference had taken place the previous Friday, April 14, at the trial in Los Angeles, and in it, for the first time Chris Darden had revealed to the defense the existence of the tapes. Here is a portion of that transcript:

DISCUSSION HELD BETWEEN THE DEPUTY DISTRICT ATTORNEYS AT SIDEBAR:

Assistant DA Chris Darden: As the court will recall, I delivered to the court several audiotapes.

The Court: Yes.

Chris Darden: And I believe the date was, I'm not sure, but I believe it was March 31. But there is a record and I ask that those audiotapes—I have no objection to the court releasing those tapes to the defense. And I'll state they are taped conversations between Mr. Kato Kaelin and his book author. In any event, these tapes relate—

The Court: Let's bring Mr. Douglas up to speed. There was a 1054.7 *in camera* [secret] hearing with the prosecution. They disclosed to the court the existence of certain tape recordings, excerpts of a statement by Kato Kaelin to an apparent book author. They were investigating Mr. Kaelin for the possibility of a number of things I would imagine and asked that they be allowed to complete their investigation before disclosing that to the defense.

Chris Darden: And, as I recall, I think I declined to suggest that Mr. Kaelin was a criminal suspect at this point, but I did ask leave of the court to have the record sealed so that I could attempt to obtain other documents that related to the audiotapes, including a book contract. Including the contract between Mr. Kaelin and Mr. Eliot and St. Martin's Press as well as the book proposal that was apparently submitted on our videotape. And so we have obtained those items and not pursuant to an SDT [subpoena], and I will turn those items over to the defense on Monday. . . .

The originals are apparently with the book author, Michael Eliot [sic] and we have copies . . . and I will also turn over to them on Monday the contract which is not signed and the book proposal.

There are inaccuracies in Darden's comments, some more potentially damaging than others. He identified me as "Michael Eliot" and said the tapes were handed over March 31 (they were handed over March 30). By far the most damaging error, however, was his saying that they had been acquired voluntarily, without subpoena. Shortly after, the press was given a copy of that transcript, and my world exploded.

Unknown to me, by late that same afternoon, I had over one hundred telephone calls on my Los Angeles phone machine by reporters from all over the country anxious to talk to me about the book I had written, the book Kato Kaelin had denied existed.

Leonard found out before I did. As soon as he began to receive calls, he phoned me at the home of a friend where I was staying and told me to get into a cab and come to his office. *Immediately.* While my driver fought through the midtown traffic Leonard called Chris Darden on the phone and all but accused him of ruining my career by misstating the fact that I had not been subpoenaed. Leonard demanded an immediate correction. Darden apologized and just before the end of that day's the court session, he went before the judge in open court:

> **Judge Ito:** (At approximately 4:00 P.M. PST): Back on the record in the Simpson matter, all parties are present. Mr. Darden, good afternoon, are you here for some reason, standing [before the microphone]?

> **Chris Darden:** To watch the trial, your honor. Beyond that, if I may, so that I may clarify a point on the record; the other day, Friday, I indicated to the court that we had recovered certain documents from Mr. Marc Eliot not by [subpoena]; in fact they were recovered by [subpoena] in lieu of our execution or obtaining a search warrant. I would like to turn over to the defense today a contract from St. Martin's Press. It involves Mr. Eliot and Kato Kaelin as well as a transcript of an interview Marc Eliot had with Kato Kaelin which apparently served as a book proposal.

In truth, three subpoenas had been issued, and along with the documents mentioned above, a number of tapes and documents had been turned over in compliance with those subpoenas.

After that, demand for an interview with me, and/or access to the tapes reached the proportions of a media frenzy. The TV and print tabloids began to throw offers of money at me. I could have made a fortune, had I wanted to go in that direction. Instead, I determined to say nothing, and to let the prosecution try their case in court. However, it was, again, Michael Plotkin, who forced me to change my course of action. Presumably besieged by the press for a comment from his golden boy, Plotkin said that yes, Kato had "explored the possibility of doing a book, but decided against it when it became plain to him at one point . . . that when you start dealing with books and you start dealing with authors' characterization of things—the fact is he just didn't want to be a party to it at that point."

I was amazed and angered. Besides trying to sidestep the obvious, Plotkin was now trying to imply that all Kato had done was "explore the possibility," when in fact a publishing contract had been sent to Plotkin, and a book had been written. When Plotkin declined to hand it in on time, the deal was effectively killed. I also resented Plotkin's suggestion that I had "characterized" Kato's words, when in fact the book was largely composed of direct quotes taken off the tapes of interviews *for which Kato had voluntarily sat.* And then, of course, there was Kato's statement in the acknowledgment section of the *completed manuscript* in which he had said the following:

I wish to thank the following people for their help and guidance during the long and difficult process of writing this book.

I have to start with Marc Eliot, whom I met at the very beginning, when the idea for this book first happened. During the course of our working together, we developed a great working relationship, and out of that a close friendship. While going over the material for this book time and time again, we managed to also share the adventures of our own present-day lives. The work proved long, intense, and difficult. The friendship forever, intense, and easy. During our downtime, we discussed at great length all the important things: women, music, careers, cars, and an unexplainable mutual desire for lousy Mexican food, not necessarily in that order. I think Marc is an incredibly talented writer, undoubtedly the best collaborator anyone could ever hope to have. . . .

I now felt I had no choice now but to go public and respond to the outrageous, misleading, and, to me, patently offensive comments of Kato and company, which in reality amounted to little more than a quite lame attempt at covering their own asses while trying somehow to shift not only the responsibility but the blame to me for Kato's performance at the trial. However, unlike my former collaborator, I chose not to sell my soul to the tabloids, and went instead on the CBS *Evening News* and NBC's *Dateline,* for no pay, to defend both the veracity of the tapes and my own integrity. (Although I didn't personally appear on any of them, the tabloids did show clips of my news appearances.) And, unlike my former collaborator, I have never forgotten that this isn't about professional promotion and personal glory, but murder.

I have therefore chosen to write this book to set the record straight, once and for all, to release the information Brian "Kato" Kaelin at first gave me so enthusiastically and then tried so hard to squelch.

What follows, then, is the whole truth, as I heard it, from Kato's mouth, about his relationship with O.J. Simpson and Nicole Brown, how he came to live in both their houses, what he stated actually took place the night of the murder, and the chain of often fantastic events that led up to and followed the grisly massacre of two young victims of a brutal cold-blooded murderer. You may think you already know all that happened in this most infamous of crimes. You don't. You may think you already know who Brian "Kato" Kaelin is. You don't. You may think you already know Nicole Brown Simpson and you may think you already know O.J. Simpson. You don't. Here, then, is the largely untold testimony of Brian "Kato" Kaelin who was a key witness in what has come to be known as the trial of the century.

2

Murder!

FROM THE TRIAL TESTIMONY OF BRIAN "KATO" KAELIN—
CALIFORNIA **v.** *O.J. SIMPSON*—**MARCH 23, 1995**
(Cross-examination):

Defense Attorney Robert Shapiro: Can you tell us
what O.J.'s life was like in January of 1994?

Brian "Kato" Kaelin: Golfing.

It had been a busy winter for

O.J. Simpson, beginning with an appearance at the 1994 Super Bowl, where he was invited to participate in the ceremonial coin toss. Life for the former-running-back legend had become largely ceremonial. During the football season, he was literally and therefore figuratively on the sidelines, reduced to providing "color" for NBC, after what may best be described as a lackluster couple of seasons as one of the men in the booth doing ABC *Monday Night Football*. The main criticism of him then was that he couldn't speak clearly enough. After a while that segued into his having nothing to say.

For the past fourteen months he had been a bachelor. His second marriage had ended in divorce, and he had tried to fill as much time as he could with travel and endorsements. Money continued to flow in, as did adulation. He could never go to a restaurant, a movie, or a gas station, without being recognized. The word *juice* floated around him like a mantra.

However, his tight circle of friends, including A.C. Cowlings and attorney Robert Kardashian, knew another side of O.J. They knew the lonely, wandering, at times angry and vengeful ex-husband of Nicole Brown. They knew a man obsessed about "reconciling" with the woman he'd known since she was seventeen and he was thirty-one. They knew about his many physical attacks on her, his increasing anger, frustration, and often-expressed need to control every aspect of her life.

For instance, he was not above spying on her when she was having sex with other men. Nor was he above sending out others to report back to him on Nicole's social activities, information he would use during fits of rage against her—even as he was busy rotating a steady cast of young, willing, sometimes married, mostly single women, including one aspiring actress named Paula Barbieri, who held out serious hope that one day she might become the third Mrs. Simpson.

It was, therefore, no surprise to his friends when O.J. invited the former houseguest of his ex-wife, one Brian "Kato" Kaelin, to move into an unused guest house at Simpson's Rockingham estate. It was, in fact, a ploy whose intent seemed quite obvious. Here was a gold mine of information for O.J., someone who had lived in his wife's guest house for a year and knew nearly every intimate move she'd made. And with whom she'd made them.

For Kato, O.J.'s rent-free offer was something of a godsend. He had spent a year living at Gretna Green, Nicole's rented house about three miles from Rockingham, and although the rent was usually about five hundred dollars a month, depending on how much baby-sitting he did—less than anyone would pay for a thin-walled one-bedroom in the seedier neighborhoods of L.A. where most of the unemployed wannabe's of the film and TV world lived—it was still a heavy ticket for the barely employed actor.

Besides, Nicole had become increasingly "dreamy" in her fantasy about all of them—herself, the two kids Sydney and Justin, and Kato—living together as a "family" in her new, smaller condo on Bundy. That really wasn't what Kato had in mind. He was, like O.J., a bachelor with a penchant for a good time. He had grown a bit weary of the constant "friendship" that had defined his life with Nicole. Especially after a confrontation in her kitchen when she openly declared her love for him—at a time she was having an affair with L.A. Raider and O.J. Simpson protégé Marcus Allen. Someone had once said if you can't stand the heat, get out of the kitchen. Kato had come to understand these words better than almost anybody. When O.J. offered a life more like King Farouk's than one of the quarter-slaves of the Egyptian potentate, it didn't take much to convince him to say yea.

The guest house at 360 Rockingham in Brentwood, California, was more like a self-contained studio apartment set in the L-shaped corner estate where Rockingham meets Ashford. The estate had two entrances, one from each cross street. The main house, through the Rockingham gate, was O.J.'s, the right wing which swung toward Ashford, was really a series of three connected guest houses, in front of which was the swimming pool, garage, and tennis courts. Kato's guest house was more like an elaborate efficiency apartment. It had a bedroom about twenty-five square feet, a small bathroom, and an adjacent office area. It had no kitchen, but Kato didn't need one. There was a common one for all three guest houses on the other side of the pool, where the tennis courts were located. Kato didn't cook, and, as he was to discover, anything in the way of food could always be found in O.J.'s well-stocked refrigerator. One of the many perks that went along with the rent-free guest house was anytime access to O.J.'s kitchen.

Kato's guest house shared a common bedroom wall with Arnelle Simpson's quarters. O.J.'s twenty-eight-year-old daughter from his first marriage, to Marguerite Simpson, lived there full-time. She and Kato had become good, but not great friends. By now he knew the meaning and wisdom of off-limits.

The last guest house belonged to Gigi, O.J.'s maid. Because she was married, most nights she would go home. When it became necessary to stay over, however, she had exclusive rights to the quarters provided by her employer.

At first, Kato didn't see all that much of O.J. For most of the winter, he was either on the road or playing golf with his regular group at the country club. They rarely socialized together.

Still, there were some terrific advantages for a struggling actor to being the houseguest of O.J. Simpson, not the least of which was that O.J. happened to be on the boards of more than a dozen entertainment-related corporations. There's a truism in Hollywood that says who you know is just as important as what you know, and in Kato's case, knowing O.J. was key. As he often told friends, "It didn't hurt to be a friend of O.J. Simpson."

**FROM THE TRIAL TESTIMONY OF BRIAN "KATO" KAELIN—
CALIFORNIA V. *O.J. SIMPSON*—MARCH 21, 1995
(Direct examination):**

Marcia Clark: Did you think it might be advantageous to you to stay with the defendant and get to know him for your acting career?

Brian "Kato" Kaelin: I didn't think that.

One of the companies on which O.J. sat was Kushner-Locke, which happened, that spring, to be producing *The

Outpost, an action movie in which Kato wanted, as he put it, "a hand up" in landing a part. As a favor to Kato, O.J. called the person in charge of casting. "Hey," O.J. told him, "my buddy Kato is coming in to read for your film. See what you can do, okay?" He was able to get into the callback readings without going through the cattle calls, just because of O.J.'s call. When Kato thanked him, O.J. simply said, "That's what friends are for."

"As I was to find out later," Kato said, "in one of those weird coincidences that tend to haunt, at approximately the same time O.J. made his call for me, Nicole, who was also a friend of the same casting people at Kushner-Locke, had called on behalf of a young actor friend of hers trying to get into the auditions, possibly for the same role. His name was Ron Goldman."

Ron Goldman, twenty-five-years-old, six-foot two inches tall, with the green-eyed easy good looks indigenous to those with their toes on the edge of the good life in Los Angeles, worked at Nicole's favorite restaurant, the Mezzaluna. He had aspirations of professional modeling and a possible acting career. Toward this end, he spent much of his spare time improving himself—his grooming, his body, and, apparently, his social status.

In a way, he had more in common with Brian "Kato" Kaelin than he had distinguishing differences. And, in the end, it was perhaps no more than the hand of fate that one benefited so enormously from his ability to seize upon the opportunity of his circumstances, while the other paid for it with his life.

For several months before his murder, Goldman had tried to ease his way into a lifestyle he found so appealing, in the person and the privilege of Nicole Brown Simpson. Several friends and witnesses recall seeing Goldman driving Nicole's red Ferrari on more than one occasion, and wondered how it was that she had come to let him use it.

The eldest of three children (a sister from his father's first marriage, a step-brother from the second wife of Fred Goldman), Goldman grew up in the Los Angeles suburb of Agoura. Early on, he showed an ability at sports and for a time earned extra money as a tennis instructor.

Although he had the look, he didn't have the luck so vital to make one's face stand out in the crowd. He did one or two print modeling jobs. His acting career consisted mostly of a one-time appearance on an early 90s TV dating show, *Studs*, and smiling broadly for his steady stream of customers, of which Nicole Simpson was among the steadiest.

Already, at the age of twenty-five, the big fear that sets in with those who have not made it yet had begun. Just over his shoulder was a new crop of actor-models, in their late teens and early twenties, pushing those ahead of them to the end of the line. By 1994, Goldman had begun considering the restaurant business as a livable, if not preferable, way to go.

His love life was uneven; one relationship he had hoped would end in marriage instead dissolved in the hedonism and heat of the California sun. It was during the last months of his life that he allowed himself to think more seriously about a liaison with Nicole. However, he had his moments of hesitation. As he told one friend, "If I ever fooled around with Nicole, O.J. would kill me."

The second week of June had been a productive one for Kato. He had just begun work on a western/action feature called *Savate*, in which he'd managed to land a small role. As happens so often in Hollywood, the connection here was personal. This time, the producer of the film, Alan Mehrez, was a friend of Kato's.

However, the aspiring actor's main source of income from the film came from working in postproduction. He was eager to learn as much as he could about the technical end of moviemaking in the hope of one day producing as well as acting. Saturday, June 11, was the first day Kato had off that week, and he was determined to enjoy it. He slept in until ten, then got dressed and went for a ten-mile run down San Vicente Boulevard, all the way to the beach and back. When he wasn't working, he averaged fifty-five miles a week, usually down San Vicente, which was a popular route among the more successful yuppie lawyers, agents, actors, and actresses who preferred the Santa Monica section of West Los Angeles, that patch of natural green and tasty boutiques that separates Brentwood from Malibu.

One of his regular rest stops along the San Vicente trail was the Fourth Street stairs, ninety-nine steps that lead down to Sunset Boulevard. The challenge is to run down them and back up. It also happens to be quite a popular pickup spot for Santa Monica's eligibles. That morning, Kato ran into two friends he usually encountered by the steps: Nicole Brown and Cora Fischman.

Kato returned to the Rockingham estate a little after twelve, took a shower, and had begun to get dressed when he noticed O.J. waving from the main house. O.J.'s living room was almost all picture windows and when the screens on Kato's door were opened, there was a clear view from one house to the other. Now, as he slipped into his jeans, he saw O.J. waving and heard the familiar boom of his voice. "Kato," O.J. screamed. This had become a familiar pattern over the months, and usually meant that the ex–football player wanted some company.

Kato left the guest house and walked the few feet to O.J.'s rear entrance. Simpson had just returned from his morning golf game and was in a talkative mood. Kato, never one to shy away from an opportunity to shoot the shit, automatically

traveled through the terrain of the refrigerator in search of a beer and who-knows-what, while O.J. casually quizzed him on what was going on. How was his week? he wanted to know.
Great.
Who was he dating?
A lot of babes. No one in particular. What about you?
The same.
Since shooting a pilot for a new TV series in which he was to play a Navy SEAL, O.J. had been around the house more than usual. His summer calendar was light, and until the start of the football preseason, when he would resume his commentary chores for NBC, O.J. Simpson really didn't have all that much to do.

He'd usually start his days playing golf and cards, either at the Riviera Country Club in Bel Air, or at any one of a number of clubs in the area that had made him an honorary member. Two weeks earlier he'd been invited by one of his regular partners, tennis pro Cory Waldman, to play thirty-six holes with President Clinton at Del Mar, near San Diego. Those were the kind of perks that went with the territory, and while O.J. was always happy to make an appearance, this was a particularly proud one for him. Golf with the President of the United States! Now, *that* was doing something. *That* was impressive. *That* was the kind of thing even Nicole would be impressed with.

Brian "Kato" Kaelin: Yes.

Robert Shapiro: And she was dating other men?

Brian "Kato" Kaelin: Yes.

Robert Shapiro: Was that a frequent occurrence to your knowledge?

Marcia Clark: Your Honor, objection.

Judge Ito: Overruled.

Brian "Kato" Kaelin: She'd go out. I don't know if it was—dating, you know, men, like, "I have a date tonight," that sort of thing. She'd go out with her friends.

Robert Shapiro: And would O.J. come over to the Gretna Green house, and visit the children?

Brian "Kato" Kaelin: Yes.

Robert Shapiro: And did he ever voice any concerns about that?

Brian "Kato" Kaelin: No.

Robert Shapiro: Did he ever show any anger or upset? Being upset at the fact that she was dating other men?

Brian "Kato" Kaelin: No.

FROM THE TRIAL TESTIMONY OF BRIAN "KATO" KAELIN—
CALIFORNIA V. *O.J. SIMPSON*—MARCH 23, 1995
(Direct examination):

Marcia Clark: I think you indicated to Mr. Shapiro on cross-examination that the defendant was never upset about Nicole dating other men. Do you recall saying that?

Brian "Kato" Kaelin: Yes.

Marcia Clark: Is that what you believe? Is that the truth, Mr. Kaelin?

Brian "Kato" Kaelin: He never let on that he was upset about her dating.

Usually by midafternoon, O.J. would be back at the house, alone, sitting around watching the big-screen TV that dominated one wall of the living room.

It occurred to Kato that lately he'd been having more and more of these informal little day chats with O.J. He began to wonder if something was bothering his famous host. After all, the weather this time of year was about as good as it got in southern L.A. What was a guy like O.J. Simpson doing sitting inside his house watching TV like a shut-in? Often during their conversations—practically every time they met it seemed to Kato—O.J. would turn away and say something similar to what he said that afternoon. "Kato, I'm so lonely. I can't stand this. I'm bored out of my mind. *There's nothing to do.*"

"God, O.J.," Kato said, "how can you be lonely? You've got it made! Look at this house! Look at those cars! Look at you!

Anything you want. Any woman." To Kato, these were the ear-marks of happiness, and O.J. should have been delirious.

"Well," O.J. said softly, "it's not like that, man. I'm just too lonely. I like hearing my kids' voices around the house, knowing they're there. I want the white picket fence, the wife, the whole dream."

It was a conversation that always made Kato a little uneasy. As far as he could tell, it was totally over between O.J. and Nicole; he'd known them both and seen too many bad things go down between them. Kato thought to himself that if O.J. was interested in that picket fence, it wasn't going to be with his ex-wife.

O.J. and Paula had already been dating for nearly two years. As he had with Nicole, O.J. began seeing the young actress while he was still married. Once Nicole had been the "other woman." Now she was the wife and it was Paula's turn to play that role. Interestingly, Kato didn't actually meet Paula until May 1994. It was as if O.J. hadn't wanted to bring Kato into that part of his life. Perhaps Nicole's friendship with him had something to do with that. Still, Kato felt he knew Paula quite well, from the way O.J. talked about her. "She was madly in love with him," Kato recalled. "When I finally did see the two of them together, I believed it, but he didn't love her. I believed that, too. He said she was eager to settle down, and to that end would do anything for him. However, to O.J., Paula was strictly a sexual partner, among the best he'd ever had. 'After I do it with her,' he told me, 'she can get me right back and ready for more. No other woman can do me like her.' He told me she was flat-out the sexiest woman he'd ever known, but that he didn't love her and had no intention of ever marrying her."

Still, Paula never brought up the question of O.J.'s fidelity, or lack of it, and all during the time of his relationship with her, he was either married to, or hoping to reconcile with,

Nicole. And, according to Kato, there were numerous others who formed a modern-day harem of sorts, there for squeezing whenever The Juice felt a little dry. "He had girls pretty much wherever he traveled. Girls he'd meet on sets. He had steady liaisons with one or two Raiderettes [Los Angeles Raider cheerleaders]. Some of them would come by regularly. I'd usually let them in the front gate. I didn't see anything wrong with it. He wasn't married, and he wasn't even engaged to Paula."

That may have been why Paula rarely stayed the night at Rockingham. That seemed fine, as O.J. had bought her a nifty little high-rise apartment on fancy Wilshire Boulevard.

When Kato first started living at O.J.'s, he would invite The Juice to come and hang with him at night, when he, Kato, was in his element. There was one dance club in Santa Monica he liked to frequent—Renaissance—and one Thursday he suggested he and The Juice go there.

Kato remembered O.J.'s face lighting up at the mention of the club's name. Although he never did go, he knew Thursday night was Nicole's "girls' night out," and knew that she and her friends also liked Renaissance. O.J. suggested Kato go ahead and "check the place out first, to see who's there." "If Nicole's there," he said, "call me and let me know." He wanted Kato to check up on her, trying to see if she was going out, and maybe with whom. That *really* made Kato uneasy, and he wound up not going to the club at all.

Now, though, O.J. seemed even more down than he'd been, especially since, as he told Kato, he was supposed to have had the kids that weekend, until Nicole had a last-minute "change of plans" and decided she was going to keep them with her.

Kato suggested they throw together a little lunch. O.J. said fine, and why didn't they spend the rest of the afternoon hanging out together at the house.

Over sandwiches, they began to discuss one of O.J.'s

favorite topics: women. At one point, O.J. turned to Kato and said, "I need to meet a nice person." Kato took the cue and before long the conversation drifted to Traci Adell. She was the current (June) *Playboy* centerfold and a friend of Kato's.

Kato had first met Traci a few months earlier at a party in her West Hollywood apartment complex. The party was taking place on the floor below hers. He looked up, saw Traci and a couple of friends on her terrace, introduced himself, and asked them to come on down. Traci and Kato hit it off and dated a few times.

He heard from her early in June when she called, all excited. The issue of *Playboy* with her in it had just hit the stands. Now, as O.J. and Kato sat in his living room and talked, Kato happened to mention that a friend of his was this month's *Playboy* centerfold, and he could introduce him to her.

O.J. kicked back on the sofa, his arms spread out, smiled, and said, "Hey, let's get a copy of the magazine, see what she looks like, and call her."

Kato volunteered to run to a nearby newsstand for a copy of the magazine. When he returned, he opened it to Traci's layout and handed it to O.J., whose initial reaction was that she wasn't his "type." She had dark hair, was about five-ten, maybe six feet. He preferred slightly smaller blondes. Kato then got Traci's phone number from his guest house. When he returned, he called for O.J., left a cute message on her machine (she was out of town making a film but asking for numbers to call back), opened a new beer, and sat down with O.J. to give the magazine a thorough going-over.

This wasn't the first time Kato had tried to introduce O.J. to women. Two sisters he knew, Lisa Marie and Susan Wilkinson, for example, were friends of Kato's who lived nearby and loved to play tennis. A few weeks earlier Kato had set up a game for all of them, and O.J. suggested they turn it into a cookout. According to Kato, O.J. didn't actually play much that day because his arthritis was acting up and his knees were bothering him. Nor was there anything particularly sexual about the day. There couldn't be, not with Paula there to "help out."

Now, as O.J. waited for Traci to call back, he decided to make a number of calls to other women. In between, the phone began ringing. Kato loved to answer, always with a funny quip and a disguised voice. "Hi," he'd say, putting on an exaggerated effeminate voice, "this is Snipper's Hair Salon, you're late for your appointment." O.J. loved it, often listening in on the extension for the caller's reaction, laughing in that silent way he had, where his head bobbed up and down and no noise came out of his mouth.

By four o'clock, when it appeared that Traci was not going to call back, O.J.'s mood shifted, and he decided to watch a little TV. He picked up the remote and began flicking from channel to channel. "Jesus," he sighed, kicking into the by-now familiar refrain. "I'm so bored, Kato. This isn't right, me sitting here inside the house on such a beautiful afternoon watching TV." You got that right, Kato thought to himself.

As O.J. flipped through the channels he'd recognize several actors and actresses he'd worked with or had met socially. Kato recalled that O.J. would say things like, "Yeah, I know her, I've been with her," or "I know that guy, he's a complete dick," or "I've been with her, she's fantastic."

One channel was running a rerun of *WKRP*. The show's star, Tawny Kitaen, had gone out with O.J. for a while. Kato knew that Nicole and Tawny didn't like each other and he was amused that O.J. stayed on that station before continuing to channel-surf.

He finally settled on the USA Channel, because it happened to be playing *The World According to Garp*. "Ever see this?" he asked Kato.

"Only bits and pieces."

"You've got to see this one part," O.J. said. According to Kato, O.J. was referring to a scene where Garp's wife was going to give head to a young guy in her car, parked in the driveway of her home. The guy comes over one last time to Garp's wife, and she says, no, no, he says one last time, so they get in the car and start. Garp, in his own car, arrives at the house and, out of force of habit, turns off his lights and coasts into the garage. Because it's raining and dark, Garp crashes into his wife's car while she's going down on her boyfriend. The force of the collision causes her to accidentally chomp off the head of her lover's penis.

Kato recalled how they watched the scene in silence. Then O.J. seemingly out of nowhere, said, "Yeah, I remember Nicole doing that with Keith [Zlomsowitch, the mâitre d' of Mezzaluna] nearly a year earlier." O.J.'s talk made Kato very uneasy. He was afraid O.J.'s mood would change. "Yeah," O.J. went on, "and the kids were home." O.J. had been outside Nicole's and seen the whole thing through her living-room window. Keith wasn't anyone she was in love with, just a friend, but it was something that bothered O.J. because it had taken place in Nicole's living room while the kids were upstairs.

Kato didn't want to hear it—Nicole was a friend of his. But Kato didn't want to challenge O.J. either. When O.J. finished the tale, he laid back, lost in thought.

To shift the mood, Kato said, "That Robin Williams sure is funny."

What finally made O.J. drop it was a phone call from Paula Barbieri. They were scheduled to attend a $25,000-a-plate charity dinner for an Israeli fund-raising organization, and Paula was calling to ask O.J. what he wanted her to wear.

When he finished talking to Paula, O.J. turned to Kato and

confessed that he really didn't want to go to the event at all. He was tired. This puzzled Kato. On the one hand, O.J. had complained all day about having nothing to do, and on the other, he had a chance to attend an event most people would have given anything to go to. "But if I have to go," he said, suddenly smiling, "I'd rather go with you, man, than Paula. At least we'd have some fun."

There had been some rough days recently between Paula and O.J., particularly after the last failed reconciliation attempt with Nicole. O.J. had given Nicole a very expensive platinum bracelet for her birthday on May 19, which, after a particularly rough fight a few days later, she had angrily returned to him. As far as she was concerned, this really was the end and she didn't want any further contact with him.

"O.J. was really angry. She didn't want him to come by her house anymore, for any reason. She was also no longer talking to him." In retaliation, O.J. threatened to turn her into the IRS, although it's unclear for what. "I think it was more of a scare tactic than anything else," according to Kato. This night, O.J. told Kato, he thought he'd give the same bracelet to Paula.

He then complained about having to take a shower and get ready, put on a tuxedo. And the $50,000 the two seats had cost him. Kato marveled at being able to spend that much money on dinner. When he asked O.J. what that felt like, he shrugged and said he did it for the PR value, that it was a good investment in his future. Making substantial donations kept his personal stock high among the corporate executives who attended these functions, many of whom would later call and hire him to make a high-paying promotional appearance. He told Kato that his appearance would eventually make him "thousands and thousands of dollars." That, he explained, was how the game worked.

After O.J. left, Kato went out with a couple of his pals, made the usual rounds, including Rebecca's, one of his favorite stops, as always in search of a new hard body to bring home. O.J. never had a problem with that. The only unbreakable rule was that Kato couldn't bring someone into the main part of the house without O.J.'s express approval. However, when it came to the guest quarters, he had complete freedom.

Unfortunately for him, the night turned out to be a bust. By 2:00 A.M., it was clear nothing was going to happen, and Kato returned to Rockingham alone. Tomorrow was Sunday. Nothing ever happened in Brentwood on Sunday. It would be a good day to relax, chill out, and take it easy before returning to work Monday morning.

Kato slept that morning until noon, unusually late even for him. When he finally dragged himself out of bed, he knew that O.J. was long gone, having gotten up early to play golf. Kato decided to take a quick run down the San Vicente trail and be back in time for the New York Knicks vs. Houston Rockets play-off game being broadcast on network TV. Basketball was in his head. After running, he returned to the guest house and changed out of his running shoes into a pair of high-tops. He intended to meet a few of his pals down at the school yard in Santa Monica where everyone goes to get into weekend pickup games. As he was tying the laces of his high-tops, he heard the familiar call of O.J.'s voice, followed by the wave of his big hand.

Kato went to the main house and was greeted by The Juice, dressed in shorts, a polo shirt, and the expensive Italian slip-ons he always wore around the house.

FROM THE TRIAL TESTIMONY OF BRIAN "KATO" KAELIN—
CALIFORNIA V. *O.J. SIMPSON*—MARCH 23, 1995
(Cross-examination):

Robert Shapiro: The first time you saw O.J. that day
[June 12], that was in the afternoon?

Brian "Kato" Kaelin: Yes.

Robert Shapiro: What time?

Brian "Kato" Kaelin: It was at, like, 2:30.

Robert Shapiro: And you had a brief conversation with
him?

Brian "Kato" Kaelin: Well, it was a conversation kind
of going off and on throughout the afternoon. But,
yeah, we were talking. And—about his golf game.
And playing cards.

Robert Shapiro: He didn't get into specifics about his
golf game or cards, did he?

Brian "Kato" Kaelin: I—he said he did good in golf.

O.J. poured Kato a glass of fresh orange juice as they small-
talked. He told Kato about the morning golf game at the
Riviera. He'd played with Craig Baumgarten and a few others,
and happened to mention that on the third hole he and Craig
had gotten into a little fight that had begun when Craig teased
O.J. over a bad shot or something, never clear about actually

what caused it. Although O.J. insisted it was only words, some of the others later told Kato that it actually became something of a fistfight, which, by the eighteenth hole, was supposedly completely forgotten. They played their usual game of poker afterward. O.J. then said he was scheduled to fly to Chicago that night to attend a Hertz function on Monday.

Kato sensed that O.J. wasn't looking forward to the midnight flight. He then put his juice down and was starting to head out when O.J. stopped him. "You ought to hang out for a while," he said. Without waiting for an answer, he flipped on the kitchen TV for the background noise he always seemed to need, and picked up the telephone receiver.

FROM THE TRIAL TESTIMONY OF BRIAN "KATO" KAELIN—
***CALIFORNIA V. O.J. SIMPSON*—MARCH 22, 1995**
(Direct examination):

Marcia Clark: Did he have another phone conversation with a woman after [Paula Barbieri] on the afternoon of June the twelfth?

Brian "Kato" Kaelin: Yes.

Marcia Clark: And who was that?

Brian "Kato" Kaelin: Traci Adell

Marcia Clark: And whose friend was that?

Brian "Kato" Kaelin: My friend.

Marcia Clark: Did you speak to Traci?

Brian "Kato" Kaelin: Briefly.

Marcia Clark: And then what did you do after you briefly spoke to Traci?

Brian "Kato" Kaelin: I handed the phone back to O.J.

(After an objection by Robert Shapiro, the direct-examination continues)

Marcia Clark: Did you hear what he said to her?

Brian "Kato" Kaelin: I didn't hear all the words. No. I tried not to listen.

"That Traci girl finally called," he said. "She left me a message. Let's call her back." Kato nodded and O.J. dialed the number. This time she picked up and they began to talk. According to Kato, she told O.J. about some of her business ideas. He offered that he was on the board of several large corporations and might be able to help her. "You know, Traci, I've got everything a man wants in the world. Everything. I've got plenty of money. I've got the beautiful home. But you know I'm just not happy. Can you make me happy?" According to Kato, O.J. looked at Kato and smiled, as if to say he was only kidding. O.J. suggested he and Traci get together in the future, and hung up. He then told Kato he'd taken a closer look at her layout in the magazine, and although she was obviously very beautiful, she wasn't his type. Still, he said on his next visit to Florida, where she was now on location, he'd make an effort to see her.

O.J. then made a series of calls to other women, many of them well-known actresses he had either dated in the past or was interested in dating. He also decided to call Jasmine Guy. O.J. had told Kato on several occasions that he wasn't into black women, with one exception, an actress by the name of Jasmine Guy.

Kato finished his juice and was about to leave. O.J., too, had to get moving. He was to attend his daughter Sydney's dance recital, scheduled to start at five that afternoon. Paula had wanted to come along, and they had been arguing back and forth about it all day on the phone. He was adamant about her not coming, because, he told her, he felt it was a family thing. Paula couldn't get over the fact that she wasn't being invited, and that annoyed O.J. even more. He just wanted to be there on his own, he told Kato. But O.J. was unable to resolve the situation, and the steady tension between him and Paula kicked up a notch.

An angry Barbieri flew to Las Vegas to spend time with singer Michael Bolton.

Kato, meanwhile, had decided to go play some basketball. He shot hoops for about an hour in Santa Monica before heading back to Rockingham. On the way he picked up a late lunch of take-out sushi from a neighborhood supermarket, which he figured to eat during the last quarter of the Knicks game. He arrived at the guest house, stretched out on the floor to give his back a rest, and flipped the TV on with the remote. A few minutes passed before he heard O.J. once again calling his name. Kato got up and saw O.J. through the screen door, waving him into the main house.

FROM THE TRIAL TESTIMONY OF BRIAN "KATO" KAELIN—
CALIFORNIA V. *O.J. SIMPSON*—MARCH 21, 1995
(Direct examination):

Brian "Kato" Kaelin: He was going to the recital. I

think . . . with Paula . . . 'cause I think O.J. just
wanted to go to the recital on his own and I think
she wanted to go . . .

Marcia Clark: Did Paula call at some point in that
afternoon during that conversation?

Brian "Kato" Kaelin: Gosh, I think so. I can't recollect it.

**FROM THE TRIAL TESTIMONY OF BRIAN "KATO" KAELIN—
CALIFORNIA V. O.J. SIMPSON—MARCH 22, 1995
(Direct examination):**

Marcia Clark: What did the defendant tell you about
Nicole at the recital? What did he tell you about
what transpired with Nicole and Sydney at the
recital?

Brian "Kato" Kaelin: About taking her or about what
she was wearing?

Marcia Clark: What did Nicole—what did the defendant tell you transpired, if anything, with regard to
himself, Nicole, and Sydney?

Brian "Kato" Kaelin: Okay, that O.J. wanted to spend
time with Sydney and that Nicole wasn't giving him
the time to have with his daughter, to talk to her at
the recital, so they went off.

Marcia Clark: Did he tell you whether he did get to
spend some time with Sydney anyway?

Brian "Kato" Kaelin: A short time.

Marcia Clark: What, if anything, did he tell you about Nicole herself at the recital?

Brian "Kato" Kaelin: About her outfit that she had on.

Marcia Clark: And what did he say about that?

Brian "Kato" Kaelin: That there weren't, who she was with, that they were wearing tight outfits and wondered if they could be grandmas and wear those outfits out.

Marcia Clark: [after a series of objections] Did you have some further conversation with him?

Brian "Kato" Kaelin: Yes.

Marcia Clark: And what was that?

Brian "Kato" Kaelin: I was, wondered if I could take a Jacuzzi.

Once in the main house, O.J. asked who won the basketball game and Kato asked O.J. how the recital went. A smile crossed O.J.'s face. "Sydney was great," he said, then the smile vanished. "But Nicole was trying to play hardball with me."

O.J. then went into a litany of complaints about what had gone wrong, beginning with the fact that Nicole had failed to save a seat for him, which resulted in his having to sit on the other side of the auditorium. After the show, he was not allowed by Nicole to visit either Sydney or Justin, and according to Kato, "he was not included and he was upset. If there was anger, it was because she wasn't going to let him see the kids." At that point, O.J. went up to Nicole and said, "What are you doing? I want to spend time with my kids. Come on, Nicole." What, he asked Kato, she can take my kids away from me now? They're my kids, too.

He also complained to Kato about what Nicole had worn to the recital. It seemed to bother him a great deal that she had on a tight, sexy black dress, which O.J. felt was totally inappropriate, not only for the dance recital, but under any social circumstances for a woman of her age. "Kato," he said, shaking his head back and forth and blowing air through his lips, "what is she going to do, wear dresses like that when she's a grandmother? Wear miniskirts? For this kind of function can't she dress like a woman? How can she dress like that for this kind of function? Why can't she dress like a proper mother? She was there with Cora Fischman, and they were dressed like they were going out to some club."

Kato tried to laugh it off. "Your relationship with her is over, isn't it?" he asked. "Who cares what Nicole wears, or how she feels about you? No matter what, you'll always have Justin and Sydney." But O.J. didn't answer. Instead, he looked away, a frown on his face.

Kato did indeed ask to use the Jacuzzi, it was for a specific purpose. Besides feeling the strain of the weekend runs and basketball games, he didn't need to hear how really upset O.J. was. "I wanted to get the conversation somewhere else," Kato recalled. "I guess in my heart I knew that something had happened at the recital." O.J. said yeah, sure, sure, in that dismissive way he has when, as Kato described it, O.J. was lost in thought. Kato stayed in the whirlpool for nearly half an hour, staring up at the sky as it turned quickly from dusk to night.

Back in his room a few minutes later, Kato heard a knock on his door. Through the screen he could see O.J., and swung it open. "Hey," O.J. said, "you know you left the Jacuzzi jets on?"

"No!" Kato felt terrible, worried he'd never be allowed to use it again.

"Are you done?"

"Yeah. I'm really sorry, O.J."

"No problem. I shut them off for you." He turned, started to leave, then stopped. "You know those two girls who came by the other night for the barbecue?"

"Sure. Susan and Lisa Marie Wilkinson."

"Right. Let's do that again. Can you set something up for Tuesday night?"

"I'll work on it," Kato said. O.J. started for the door again. Kato could no longer ignore the weird vibes in the room. "Everything all right, O.J.?"

"Yeah, sure." O.J. closed the door behind him as he left. Kato wondered just how lonely he was, to want to bring back the Wilkinson girls, in whom he'd shown no real interest.

Kato thought it would be a good thing at least to call them and pass along the invitation. He got one of the Wilkinsons on the phone and she said she'd have to check with her sister, but that Tuesday sounded like it might be okay.

Apparently, around this time, (approximately 7:35 P.M.), O.J. called Gretchen Stockdale, a former Los Angeles Raiderette, and left the following message: "Hey, Gretchen, sweetheart, it's Orenthal Jones, who is finally at a place in his life where he is, like, totally, totally unattached with everybody . . . Ha . . . haaah! Uh, in any event, umm, I've got a Sunday evening, uh, I'd love . . . I guess I'm catching a red-eye at midnight or something to Chicago, but I'll be back Monday night. . . . "

About the same time, Kato had called his friend Tom O'Brien, who was, at the time, a district attorney in San Diego. Kato and Tom had been friends since the fourth grade, and had grown up together in Milwaukee. They spoke on the phone several times a week, rarely about anything special. While Kato was talking to O'Brien, O.J. came back and signaled for him to hang up, which he did.

FROM THE TRIAL TESTIMONY OF BRIAN "KATO" KAELIN—
CALIFORNIA V. *O.J. SIMPSON*—MARCH 22, 1995
(Direct examination):

Brian "Kato" Kaelin: I gave him the money and he said he was going to get a hamburger and I said, "Can I go?"

Marcia Clark: You invited yourself to go with him?

Brian "Kato" Kaelin: Yes.

Marcia Clark: And what was his response to that?

Brian "Kato" Kaelin: Sure.

Marcia Clark: He seemed real excited to have you come?

Robert Shapiro: Objection.

Judge Ito: Sustained.

Brian "Kato" Kaelin: Wouldn't you? (Laughter)

"Kato," O.J. said, "I've got an embarrassing question to ask you."

"What is it?" Kato flashed on somehow having really screwed up the Jacuzzi.

"I have all hundreds. Can I borrow five dollars to give the skycap at the airport?"

"Sure," Kato said, greatly relieved to hear that that's all it was. He pulled out a twenty, the smallest bill he had. O.J. put it in his pocket and said he was going to get something to eat. Without thinking, Kato blurted out, "You mind if I come along? Can I go?"

Kato: "He paused, it seemed, for a while. He looked at me in a very odd way. His stare made me feel as if I had been out of line to invite myself along. In my head I'm thinking, and I've thought so many times since, *'I wasn't supposed to go.'* I had invited myself and felt uncomfortable about it. I was about to say, 'You know what, on second thought I'm not really hungry,' but before I could, he said, 'Yeah, sure, come along, we'll grab a burger or something.'"

They went outside, got into O.J.'s Bentley, and headed for a McDonald's.

When they came to a stoplight at Twenty-sixth and San Vicente, Kato glanced over and noticed again how tired O.J. appeared. He suggested that he might want to take a nap before heading out later that night. O.J. responded in short, monosyllabic answers. According to Kato's testimony, he, Kato, then looked at the clock, at either 9:15 or 9:18, to notice what time it was, unable to explain just why he did so. However, Kato told me he had no trouble remembering the exact time being 9:18. He even remembers the exact place to match the time, where San Vicente crosses Twenty-sixth Street, at the stoplight. The reason for this precision, according to

Kato, was because O.J., not Kato, had checked the time, and made a point of having Kato confirm it.

"No time," O.J. said. He then looked at the car clock. "Is that right?"

Kato then verified the time for O.J., thereby setting the time frame in both their heads. It remains unknown if anyone has, to date, checked the accuracy of that clock, or gone over it to see if anything was done about resetting it, either before or after that Sunday.

When they arrived at McDonald's, Kato figured that since O.J. only had large bills, he, Kato, would pick up the tab for the dinner. "Let me pay for this," he said, and handed O.J. another twenty.

O.J., who had been quiet the whole ride, said nothing while going through the drive-in. O.J. was in the same mood he'd been in for a while, which made Kato increasingly uncomfortable. O.J. ordered the largest burger they had and a Coke. Kato, who rarely eats breads or fried or fast foods, wasn't a frequent customer of McDonald's, but since he was there with The Juice, ordered a chicken sandwich, french fries, and a large orange soda.

Kato remembered two Spanish people working the windows, a man and a woman. He thought a glimmer of recognition crossed the woman's face. O.J. paid her with Kato's twenty, then handed him back his change. "I hate to do this to you, Kato," he said. Kato wasn't sure what he meant, until O.J. took Kato's food out of the bag, tossed it to him, and wolfed his own down in "no seconds flat." Kato sat there holding his still-wrapped food and drink, deciding that except for a few fries sticking out of the bag, he'd be better off eating it back at the house.

As they drove back to the house, O.J. continued in silence, as if thinking about something, staring into space. By this time, according to Kato, he was so uncomfortable he didn't even ask O.J. for his straw. After a while, Kato tried to small-talk. O.J. remarked he hated taking the red-eye flight. Kato then asked if he could use the typewriter in the little office that adjoined his room. "That's Nicole's," O.J. said. "But it's okay. Go ahead and use it."

"What airline are you flying out on?"

"I don't know, man . . . I think American . . ."

"What's the trip for, again?"

"Some Hertz thing . . ."

By now, Kato was sure he wasn't supposed to speak and it made him uneasy. When they arrived back at the house, O.J. pulled into the Ashford gate, and parked the Bentley by the garage.

FROM THE TRIAL TESTIMONY OF BRIAN "KATO" KAELIN—
CALIFORNIA V. O.J. SIMPSON—MARCH 22, 1995
(Direct examination):

Marcia Clark: When you got back to Rockingham and the defendant parked the car in the location you indicated on People's 136, can you tell us, sir, what happened next?

Brian "Kato" Kaelin: I got out of the car and I had my food, and I walked toward the kitchen and I thought I was kind of inviting myself, so I turned and I went to my room.

Marcia Clark: (after locating the action on a series of photographs, using the telestrator) When you got to that location, what did you do?

Brian "Kato" Kaelin: When I got to that [O.J.'s kitchen] door?

Marcia Clark: Yes.

Brian "Kato" Kaelin: I turned.

Marcia Clark: Okay. And what did you see?

Brian "Kato" Kaelin: O.J.

Marcia Clark: And where was he?

Brian "Kato" Kaelin: At the driver's side door of the Rolls [sic].

Marcia Clark: Did you say anything to him?

Brian "Kato" Kaelin: No.

Marcia Clark: What did you do?

Brian "Kato" Kaelin: I looked and said, "I'll eat in my room."

Marcia Clark: And what did you do then?

Brian "Kato" Kaelin: I took off, to my room, to eat—

Marcia Clark: Did he make any response to you when you said, "I'll eat in my room."

Brian "Kato" Kaelin: Oh, no, that was in my mind— "I'll eat in my room."

Marcia Clark: You didn't say that out loud?

Brian "Kato" Kaelin: No. No. In my head, I was going, "I'll eat in my room." Sorry.

Marcia Clark: Did he say anything to you?

Brian "Kato" Kaelin: No.

Marcia Clark: Did you say anything to him?

Brian "Kato" Kaelin: No.

Kato got out of the car and walked to the main-house door that leads to the kitchen, waiting for O.J. to open it. He turned to look for him and saw him standing by the front driver's side door of the Bentley, about ten yards from the front of his house. Kato was going to have his dinner in the main house, but when he saw that O.J. was standing at the door of the Rolls-Royce, he said "I'll eat this in my room."

"He wasn't walking to the house," Kato recalled. "I started for my room. He didn't say anything or make a move. He gave me a look that said, 'What are you doing?' Just before I went inside [to my guest house], I turned and saw that he was still standing next to the Bentley. I never saw him go into the house, and kept wondering to myself why he didn't.

"I don't know why, but this entire night, I kept having the feeling that something was not right. It just wasn't right."

Kato went into his room, started eating and, according to

telephone records, at 9:45, decided to call back Tom, in San Diego, to complete the conversation that had been interrupted when O.J. had come into his room to borrow some cash and they wound up getting a bite to eat. Kato couldn't resist teasing Tom about having had dinner with O.J. Simpson; they both laughed a little and Kato hung up. He finished his food and decided to try to do a little work. He wanted to use Nicole's typewriter to update his résumé.

The office is on the other side of a set of double doors that lead to the main house, which can only be unlocked from O.J.'s side. When Kato turned on the office lights he couldn't help but see how eerie the reflection was through the window. Again he felt uneasy. If anyone were outside, how hard would it be for them to look in?

It was ten o'clock when he sat down at the IBM Selectric, turned it on, and discovered it didn't seem to be working. He thought perhaps the outlet was bad, and tried every one in the room. The result was the same.

He went back to his bed and tried to figure out what to do next. He decided to call a friend of his, Rachel Ferrara.

Kato had met Rachel on the set of *Savate.* She was a production assistant, or glorified gofer. They'd hit it off, dated a few times, and on more than one occasion spent the night together at the Rockingham guest house. He dialed her number, and when she answered the phone, he began to feel a little better. After a few minutes he put on one of his funny voices and described how frustrated not being able to work on his résumé made him feel.

Rachel suggested she could unfrustrate him if he came over to her place. He thought about it for a few minutes before deciding no, he had to make an attempt to get *something* productive done that night. He put the phone receiver down and once again tried the outlets for the typewriter, this time putting

on a bit of a show for Rachel on the other end. "I'M PLUG-
GING IT IN HERE BEHIND THE DESK . . . NOTHING . . .
I'M PLUGGING IT IN HERE BEHIND THE LAMP . . .
NOTHING . . . " He finally gave up, turned the adjacent office
lights off, sat back on the bed, picked up the receiver, and continued talking to Rachel, who once again suggested he come
over to her place.

FROM THE TRIAL TESTIMONY OF BRIAN "KATO" KAELIN— *CALIFORNIA V. O.J. SIMPSON*—MARCH 22, 1995 (Direct examination):

Marcia Clark: During that phone call, sir, did something unusual occur?

Brian "Kato" Kaelin: Yes.

Marcia Clark: And what was that?

Brian "Kato" Kaelin: I heard a thumping noise. . . . I
was on the phone still and was talking to Rachel and
I said to Rachel, I asked her, "Did we just have an
earthquake?"

At about 10:40 Kato heard the now-famous "noises," a
series of three thumps as he described them. "It sounded as if,
I thought in my head, 'Someone's back there,' but I wanted to
believe instead we had an earthquake." Which is exactly what
he asked Rachel, if they'd just had an earthquake. He was hoping she would say they had, but she didn't.
   "'Well,' I told her, 'this is so weird. The picture hanging on

the wall opposite my bed just moved.' It was a big, poster-sized, framed picture of flowers, and was now completely tilted to one sidé. 'And I heard this funny noise . . .'"

Rachel repeated that she knew for certain there had been no earthquake.

For Kato, it was a weird night. "In my head I knew someone was back there in the alley behind the house." He told Rachel he was going to check things out.

Kato had a small penlight he kept next to his bed ever since the big earthquake the previous January. Michelle, O.J.'s former maid, had given it to him. It wasn't very big, or bright, but the only one available. He thought he would take it along with him. He told Rachel, "If I'm not back in ten minutes, start to worry."

"Thanks a lot," she said, laughing. "Now I *will* worry . . . "

He hung up, stepped outside the room, and ran the three steps that led to the main path that circled the entire house. He followed it to the front lawn, and that's when he noticed for the first time the limo outside the Ashford gate, which meant that O.J. must not yet have left for the airport. "I didn't actually see anyone in the limo," Kato recalled later, "but still felt a little safer just knowing it was there. I also saw Chachi, O.J.'s black chow, hanging out on the front lawn."

Kato then proceeded to the end of the garage, where a wrought-iron gate led to a long, narrow pathway behind the main house that extends its entire length, past his guest house, Arnelle's, and the maid's quarters.

The gate was broken off its hinges. Kato picked it up, moved it out of the way, stepped into the pathway, and says he decided not to go very far. It was pitch-black out—no lights—and the little penlight proved useless. He figured if someone were still back there, it might not be such a great idea to confront him. For whatever reason, he says he went no farther.

Kato Kaelin: The Whole Truth

FROM THE TRIAL TESTIMONY OF BRIAN "KATO" KAELIN—
***CALIFORNIA* V. *O.J. SIMPSON*—MARCH 22, 1995**
(Direct examination):

Marcia Clark: And so you were able to see the area of the walkway that was right behind your room?

Brian "Kato" Kaelin: No.

Marcia Clark: Was that in darkness?

Brian "Kato" Kaelin: Yes.

Marcia Clark: After—and you stopped at that point?

Brian "Kato" Kaelin: Yes, I did.

Marcia Clark: Why?

Brian "Kato" Kaelin: Well, I figured I'd just give up. I didn't want to investigate anymore.

Instead, he returned to the front of the house and was relieved to see the limo still there, although he was not sure why O.J. hadn't let it in. There was an intercom system installed for that very purpose, and Kato was sure the driver would have been instructed to buzz upon his arrival.

Kato went to the gate and pushed the inside button that activated it. The gate opened, the limo came through the entrance and around the loop that leads to the Rockingham gate. When the driver was directly in front of the main entrance to O.J.'s house, he turned his engine off and got out.

Kato introduced himself and asked if he was there to take O.J. to the airport. He confirmed that he was. Kato then asked if he thought they'd had an earthquake. The driver said he didn't think so. Kato told him about the strange noises, and that his picture had moved.

As they talked Kato noticed O.J.'s golf bag in front of the main entrance to his door. Usually, Kato knew, when O.J. expected a limo, he put his things out front for the driver to load. It flashed through his mind that he didn't remember seeing the clubs when he first came out to investigate, then dismissed it as a probable oversight on his part.

The driver then popped open the trunk of the limo and put the clubs in. Kato asked if he'd seen O.J. The driver said no. "I hope he didn't oversleep," Kato said, figuring O.J. must have taken that nap. "I don't want him to miss his flight." He felt better knowing O.J. was still in the house, and decided to take one more look down the pathway. He returned to the broken iron gate, went a little farther in, saw and heard nothing, and returned once more to the limo.

When he got there, he saw O.J.

Kato didn't know where he'd come from. Seemingly out of nowhere while he, Kato, was investigating the noises.

O.J. said he'd overslept. Later on, the limo driver said he saw someone he thought might have been O.J. going through the front door into the house.

"It was then that I noticed for the first time a blue duffel bag with a patch of leather on it, like a knapsack, on a little plot of grass next to the back right rear taillight of the Bentley, about fifteen feet behind and to the side of the limo. I didn't remember seeing it before, and couldn't understand why it was there, since O.J.'s luggage usually is where the golf clubs had been. This made no sense, I told myself."

O.J. was now standing between the Bentley and the limo.

Kato called to him and said, "Don't forget this bag," and started to go for it.

"No, no, I'll get it," Kato recalled O.J. saying. "He came all the way over, past me, to the Bentley. My heart started pounding. Like so many things that night, this didn't make any sense. I turned away and never saw exactly what happened to it. There are three possibilities. He either picked it up and brought it into the main house, put it in the trunk or one of the seats of the Bentley, or he put it in the limo. If he did that, he had to have put it in the backseat with him, because the trunk of the limo was closed and would have had to be reopened from inside, which it wasn't. . . . I think he got into the limo with the bag."

In any case, the bag was never seen again.

FROM THE TRIAL TESTIMONY OF BRIAN "KATO" KAELIN—
CALIFORNIA v. *O.J. SIMPSON*—**MARCH 22, 1995**
(Direct examination):

Marcia Clark: Did you have a conversation with the defendant when you saw him there [outside the house waiting for the limo to be loaded]?

Brian "Kato" Kaelin: Yes.

Marcia Clark: What did you say?

Brian "Kato" Kaelin: Well, at some—I was telling him about this noise I heard. I said, "O.J., I heard this noise and I thought it was an earthquake and I thought maybe someone's back there," and I told him I was going to investigate it and I had a lousy flashlight.

Marcia Clark: And then what?

Brian "Kato" Kaelin: And so I asked the limo driver, I said, "Do you have a better flashlight?" And he checked and he looked around and he didn't, and then I said, "O.J., do we have a better flashlight?" and he—when I told him about the noise he was going to take one way, I was going to go another way, but that's when I said, "Well, we have this lousy flashlight. We need another one," and so he was going to go inside and check.

Marcia Clark: And then what happened next?

Brian "Kato" Kaelin: Okay. So we went into the house. I followed behind, and he got toward the kitchen area, and I was kind of in the front-door entrance behind him but not yet in the kitchen, it was—I didn't look, but he said, "Oh, it's that late," so we didn't have time and he—we didn't get the flashlight, so he had to catch the flight.

"O.J.," Kato said, "I heard this noise behind my room. It kind of spooked me. I thought we'd had an earthquake, but I guess we didn't. I'd like to take another look around."

O.J.'s eyes lit up and his head went back, as if he were surprised.

"You did? You heard noises behind the house?"

"Yes. Maybe someone's trying to break in or something."

"Well, we better check on it! I'll go one way around the house and you go the other way."

To Kato, this seemed extremely odd behavior which he would later describe as "bad acting." "In my head I said to myself, 'Why? I don't understand, a minute ago O.J. was rushing to make his flight. Now, suddenly, he wants to search the premises.' I suggested we'd need a better flashlight. I asked the limo driver if he had one. He looked in the glove compartment and said no, he didn't. I asked O.J. if there was one in the house."

"I think so. Let me check."

Kato followed O.J. inside the house, to the kitchen. Later on, Kato would say that he "knew" O.J. wasn't going to get a flashlight, by his reactions. He suddenly looked up at the wall clock and said, "Whoa, is that the time? I've got to go."

Kato also looked at the clock. It was 11:15. As they both left through the front door O.J. suddenly turned to Kato and said, "Okay, put the alarm on."

Kato said he didn't know the code. And wondered why O.J. would ask him to, since they both knew Kato didn't know it. The only people who did were Arnelle, who had gone out for the evening, and Gigi, the maid, to whom O.J. had given the night off.

"Okay," O.J. said. "I'll do it."

"Hurry up," Kato said. "You don't want to miss your flight."

They said good-bye and O.J. slid into the back of the limo. He put his arms behind his head, leaned back and let out a slow, steady blast of air from between his lips. Kato asked the driver if he was going to make it.

"I'll make it," he said. Kato shut O.J.'s door, went to the side of the gate, pushed the button, and let them out. As the limo passed him he gave O.J. a thumbs-up sign, unsure if he could see it through the car's heavily tinted windows.

After Kato watched the car disappear down the road, he started back for his guest house. But when he passed O.J.'s front door, he noticed the alarm hadn't been set. Kato was concerned about that. He feared, quite logically, that if there had been someone behind the house, in the pathway, that person might have been able to slip inside the house while the limo was pulling out of the gate, or that O.J. would be angry at him, if someone did break in.

Kato went to his place and decided to call Rachel back. He got her on the phone and said again how weird this night continued to be. Fifteen minutes into their conversation, the call-waiting beep went off. Kato hit the button and the next voice he heard was O.J.'s. He wasn't sure where he was calling from, and didn't ask.

"Kato, it's O.J. I forgot to set the alarm. Let me give you the codes."

O.J. gave him the numbers and explained how to punch them in. Kato was a bit "freaked," as he put it, to have to go back outside, but he agreed to do it. He hung up, told Rachel he'd call her back, and stepped out his front door, up three steps to the pathway and walked the fifteen feet to O.J.'s front door to activate the alarm. When he finished, Kato ran back to his room, closed the door, and turned the lock. With Gigi gone, it was the first time he'd ever been completely alone in the house.

Now, Kato wondered, how could O.J. forget to set the alarm? And perhaps more importantly, why? "When the call-waiting call came in, after twenty minutes [e]lapsed, I wondered why O.J. suddenly remembered in the limo? If it was important enough to call me back about the alarm, why didn't he do it in the first place? I thought about if he hadn't set the alarm, someone could have come in and left."

Kato then called Rachel back one more time, talked to her until about 1:30. She could tell he was agitated, and once more urged him to come over to spend the night. The offer sounded even better this time, except that now Kato was afraid to open his door for any reason.

He hung up, stretched out on his bed, and began to read the

Sunday Calendar section of the *Los Angeles Times*. After a while he heard the clacking of high heels on the walkway and figured it was Arnelle. *Hoped* it was Arnelle. He read for a few more minutes, turned his lights off, and tried to sleep.

He didn't get much, if any. He kept tossing and turning all night, unable to get the strange events of the evening out of his mind. "At one point," he recalled, "I kept hearing O.J.'s phone ringing and thought I must be dreaming. When it was really quiet, from my room I could hear the soft, high *brrr* of O.J.'s phone from the main house. It seemed to ring a thousand times that night." He didn't know at the time, but at least one of those calls was probably from O.J. Simpson, trying desperately to get hold of Kato before the police did. According to phone records and the police, there were at least four completed phone attempts from O.J. at 7:04 A.M. and again at 7:28 A.M., Chicago time, (5:04 and 5:28, Los Angeles time) the morning following the murders.

Most of the other calls were from the security service and the police, desperately trying to find out if anyone was home.

And still alive.

Three questions related to this series of events demand if not immediate answers, then merit additional investigation. The first is, if you are O.J. Simpson, and your house guest informs you he heard noises behind the house and suspects it might be a prowler, your daughter lives on the premises, and you are leaving to travel two thousand miles away, why don't you simply call the police? Apparently no one, O.J., Kato, not even the limo driver, ever thought this the most logical or safest thing to do.

The second is, under these circumstances, how could anyone possibly forget to turn on the security system? I have one in my own home, and it is as second nature to me as turning out the lights when I leave.

The nagging, unanswered question remains, why did O.J. forget, resulting in a twenty-minute gap of security. One possible explanation is chilling. Leaving the house "unsecured" for nearly twenty minutes gives someone sufficient time to enter, or leave, unnoticed, unclocked, unrecorded. For what purpose? Perhaps to remove a blue duffel bag that may have been left behind? If such a person did manage to slip in or out that night, his (or her) actions might easily have allowed O.J. to forget about calling the police, even as his limo barreled toward the airport.

Finally, and perhaps most shocking, Kato's admission of having gone behind the house, to the pathway where he believed he heard a prowler, establishes, for the first time, a third person in close enough proximity to the still-unexplained "bloody glove." There is, of course, the person who dropped it, and, presuming he didn't plant it—which would entail a conspiracy unlike any other in modern police history—Detective Mark Fuhrman, the much-put-upon officer who discovered the glove.

Now there is also Kato Kaelin, who admits to having gone unaccompanied to the immediate vicinity where the glove was eventually found, *hours before the police first arrived.* The implications of Kato's "spontaneous investigation" continue to loom large in the realm of the as-yet-unreconcilable series of increasingly bizarre facts that surround the O.J. Simpson murder trial.

Perhaps even more unbelievably, this was not the first time Kato had been on that pathway. Just two weeks before the murder, during Memorial Day weekend, Arnelle and Jason had thrown a party, during which Arnelle twice locked herself out of her guest house. Inexplicably, both times she asked, of all those there, Kato, one of the physically largest people, to go behind her quarters, on the pathway, and climb into her room through the open window to get her keys. Kato was, therefore, not only familiar with the area that was to play such a crucial role in the entire trial, but had been there on at least three separate occasions, prior to Mark Fuhrman. At least twice, Kato was close enough to the actual area where the glove was found to have trampled the grounds, and climbed through the window of the adjoining guest house. That none of this has been brought up in court is nothing less than shocking.

Brian "Kato" Kaelin was awakened at dawn by an urgent pounding on his door. As he opened his eyes he heard a voice say, "Police."

The wooden vertical window slats rattled from the pounding, a noise startling enough to awaken him fully.

He had no idea what as going on. Having had at best a fitful night's sleep, he wondered if he was really awake at all, or in the grip of some dark dream.

He shifted the door window's wooden slats and looked out. In the charcoal gray of the predawn, he could see the figure of a man standing at the bottom of the three steps that led down to his entrance off the pathway. Behind him all he could see were six official-looking legs.

The four men were dressed in plainclothes—suit coats and ties. None of them flashed a badge. Kato shouted, "Hold on," grabbed a T-shirt—he'd slept in the bottom half of his pajamas—and tentatively opened the door.

"Who are you?" the one at the bottom of the steps said.

"Kato. I live here, in this house."

Detective Mark Fuhrman was the first to walk into the room. The three others, Detectives Vannatter, Lange, and

Phillips stayed behind, but stepped down to the bottom, level with the entrance to the guest house.

"What's going on?"

The first one asked again who he was. "My name's Kato Kaelin," he repeated. "This is where I live."

The detective stared into Kato's bloodshot eyes. After a few seconds of silence, the detective asked him if he'd done drugs the night before.

"I don't do drugs." At that point, Kato, having shaken the webs off his brain, began to wonder what was going on. He flashed on O.J.'s plane having crashed. "What happened?" he asked the detective, who ignored the question and offered one of his own instead.

"What did you wear last night?"

Kato knew now that something was definitely wrong, but still had no idea what. He pointed to the pants he'd worn and laid over the chair, and a pair of black Doc Marten's work shoes.

The detective picked them up. "These the boots you wore last night?"

Kato was about to say something when he noticed one of the other detectives outside move his hands to his hips, which caused the jacket he was wearing to part slightly. There, glinting in the early light, was a badge attached to his belt.

The detective in the room took a small flashlight from his pocket and said he was going to give Kato an examination, something he called a Horizontal Nysphagmus Gaze Test, a check to see if Kato had, in fact, taken any drugs the evening before. He shined the penlight directly into Kato's eyes and, while doing so, said, "Your eyes are really red. Did you smoke some pot last night?"

"No," Kato repeated to Detective Fuhrman. He repeated that he never used drugs, and explained he had a chronic red-eye condition that worsened with a lack of sufficient sleep.

When Fuhrman completed the test, which proved negative, Kato turned to all four men and said, "Come on, fellas, what's—what's going on?"

According to Kato, they seemed a little annoyed that he was asking that question. They let it be known that they were there to interrogate him, not the other way around.

"Anything unusual happen last night? What did you do last night?"

Kato told them he'd spent the night at home and made a few phone calls. Later on (in what may prove to be a major victory for the defense's theory of a police conspiracy), he told me he could not clearly remember who first brought up the thumping on the walls. According to Kato, he was going to insist on his rights, but didn't because he felt he had nothing to hide. He asked what was going on, and claims not to remember saying anything about the noises behind the house to Detective Fuhrman. Later on, Marcia Clark would insist he did. Kato's first clear memory of saying anything about it was to Vannatter, when they were already outside the house. "I believe, for some reason, they needed to prove I said it first," Kato told me. "I could have, though. I don't know."

Another officer asked Kato if he had any cuts on his hands or feet. He said no.

Fuhrman then asked if he could look around. Kato showed him the modest quarters and even though he seems unsure of when he first mentioned the thumps, pointed out the picture, still tilted from the force of the thumps, and the typewriter that hadn't worked.

One of them asked if it were possible to get into the main house from there. Kato told him the doors in the office could only be opened from O.J.'s side.

"Who else lives here?" Fuhrman asked.

"Arnelle Simpson. O.J.'s daughter."

"Is she home?"

"I think so. Her room is right next to mine." Fuhrman asked how Kato knew she was home, and he said he thought he'd heard her footsteps earlier in the morning.

At that point, Fuhrman led Kato outside while Vannatter and Lange began to pound on Arnelle's door. It seemed to Kato the pounding went on forever, and he began to wonder if something had happened to her, and maybe that was why the police were there.

Finally, one of the detectives turned to Kato and asked, "Are you sure she's here?"

"I think so . . ."

Arnelle suddenly swung her door open. "What's this all about?" she asked Kato.

"I don't know," he said. "These fellows are detectives. Is O.J. okay?"

Before she could answer, Detective Lange asked Kato if he knew who Nicole was.

"Sure," he said. "O.J.'s ex-wife."

"How well do you know her?"

"She's a friend."

"Did O.J. see her last night?"

"I don't believe so. He went to the airport."

"Where did he go?"

"Chicago. To a Hertz convention or something."

Detective Vannatter then came over and asked Kato if he had a phone number where O.J. could be reached. He didn't.

Arnelle excused herself, went back into her guest house, and got dressed. When she reemerged, she asked again what this was all about.

The detectives made sure Arnelle and Kato didn't get too close to each other, to prevent them from having any private conversations. One of the detectives then asked Arnelle if she had keys to the main house. She said she did and went back inside to get them. When she returned, Vannatter said, "Both of you come with us," signaling to Lange to come with him. They went up to the door to the main house, about fifteen feet from Kato's room. Once inside, they went past the bar/pool table den area, which O.J. had converted into a personal trophy room. The entire place was filled with photos of him and other celebrities, and, of course, O.J.'s impressive array of awards, the center-piece of which was his 1968 Heisman Trophy.

Detective Lange asked Kato if he'd ever driven O.J.'s Bronco. He said no. Lange then asked if there were a set of spare keys for it in the house. Kato said he thought they were probably in the kitchen. Everyone started searching for them. At one point, Kato found a ring of keys, held them up, and said, "I'm not sure if these are for the Bronco."

One detective took the keys, and Vannatter escorted Kato back to the bar area and told him to have a seat. The distance was far enough away from the kitchen, on the other side of the dining room, so that although Kato could still hear Arnelle's voice, it was muffled and mingled with those of the detectives.

Vannatter pulled out a pad and pen and began to question Kato, repeating the same ones they'd been asking since they'd first knocked on his door. When it came to the "thumping noises," Kato asked if Vannatter thought they meant anything. The detective shook his head no and turned away. Kato then went on to describe the scene with the limo driver, the duffel bag, O.J.'s leaving, O.J.'s calling to set the alarm, all of it except the full extent of his search behind the pathway. Curiously, the search didn't seem to get as much attention as the rest.

Suddenly Arnelle's voice rose, loud and clear through the house, a wailing, terrifying cry. "I have to call Al," she screamed.

She ran to a telephone and called O.J.'s close friend, Al Cowlings, otherwise known as A.C. It seemed only a matter of moments before he showed up at the front door. Everyone then convened in the living room, and the detectives officially announced what was going on. Nicole had been murdered.

Arnelle began weeping softly. Kato went to hold her, and as he did so all the strange events of the previous night began to play off each other in his head. "I kept telling myself I knew this was a weird night and now it was all making sense to me. . . ."

Through her tears, Arnelle asked the detectives if Nicole's family had been informed. They said no. She volunteered to make the call. The group was escorted back to the kitchen area and stood around the center preparation block as Arnelle dialed the Brown home.

"Judi," she said shakily to Nicole's mother, then broke down, unable to continue. Detective Lange took the receiver from her and introduced himself, after which he said, "I'm sorry to have to tell you that your daughter Nicole has been murdered."

It was that cut-and-dry. After a long pause, during which Mrs. Brown began to cry, Lange said softly, "I'm sorry." A few seconds later he added, "The children are okay." He then told Mrs. Brown the police had them at the station, and that he would see to it they were brought to her.

The other detectives continued to look around the house. After Lange hung up, Arnelle and A.C. who had volunteered to help with the children, left with one of the detectives for the police station, to retrieve them. When they were gone, Vannatter resumed his questioning of Kato.

He began again with the events of the night before, and asked one more time if Kato had ever used drugs. Kato told him what happened, and denied ever smoking even a cigarette. Vannatter asked several questions about his background, where he was from, what he did for a living, what his duties were around the house. All the while, Kato kept thinking, to himself, Nicole's dead, Nicole's dead, and that they thought O.J. might have actually had something to do with it.

Kato asked if he could get dressed, as he was still in his pajamas and T-shirt. Vannatter said okay and escorted him back to his room. When they returned to the main house, Justin and Sydney were there. Arnelle, A.C., and Lange had brought them back from the Bundy police station.

It was clear the kids had no idea at this time what was going on. Sydney lay down on a small daybed near a coffee table in the breakfast nook of the kitchen, clutching her security blanket against her face and sucking her fingers, habits she'd had for as long as anyone could remember.

Justin, always a bit hyper, now seemed confused, as if he didn't understand why he was at his father's house. When he saw Kato, his face brightened up. "Streets of Rage," he shouted, and held up a game cartridge he had been carrying around with him. He ran to the TV set in the kitchen next to the breakfast nook, plugged it in, and started playing. Kato joined him.

Sydney started calling for her mommy and at one point got off the daybed, went to the phone, and dialed her home number.

"Kato," she suddenly shouted, "there's a strange man answering the phone at Mommy's house! Who is that man?"

"There must be some kind of mix-up at the phone company," he said.

Satisfied with that answer, she yawned and lay back down.

The detectives continued to search the kitchen, every so often asking Kato another question. When they'd want to speak to him about something, they'd motion him to move to the bar area. Justin then got up and shouted for Kato to sit down and continue playing the game.

This time one of the detectives whispered quietly, but loud enough for Kato to hear, "Let's take him down to the station for an interview."

They explained to him that the house was about to get crazy, and it would probably be better if they could talk in a more controlled environment. Whatever that meant, Kato thought to himself. One of them turned and said, "Okay, Kato. Outside. Two uniforms will come by and drive you to the station." For the first time Kato realized he was actually being considered as a suspect.

Detective Lange and one of the others took him through the living room to the front door. They walked deliberately when, without warning, one of them took Kato by the arm and said, "Watch out for the blood on the floor."

Kato looked down suddenly and said, "Oh . . . " Indeed, there were several drops of blood directly in front of his feet. Now Kato flashed on how he had been asked so many times if he had any fresh cuts on his hands, face, or body. "I could see their eyes once more moving over my exposed skin, as if searching for any open wounds."

The floor of O.J.'s living room is done in wide, birch-colored planks, with flat, round imitation peglike markings alternating in a dark and light brown pattern. It occurred to Kato, and obviously the police, that if anyone had tried to clean up freshly spilled blood, they could easily have missed some, as it blended so easily into the intricate markings. In his head, Kato began to put more pieces together.

He took a deep breath and tiptoed around the blood, keeping his eyes fixed to the floor so as not to accidentally step in any until he was outside. "I could not believe what I had just seen."

It was now 7:30 A.M. The detectives had been at the house for nearly two hours. A parked black-and-white was just outside the Rockingham gate. One of the two uniformed policemen got out and came over to where Kato, Lange, and Vannatter were standing. He was Spanish. The other had a British accent. He informed Kato he was there to take him to the station.

Just then, Jason came barreling along Ashford in his Jeep and pulled up in front of the gate. He got out and went to Arnelle, who was by now also standing outside the house. "What's going on?" he kept wanting to know.

Arnelle put her arms around him and said, "Oh my God, they're trying to pin this on Dad! They're trying to pin this on Dad! I can't believe it!" She broke down completely and began to sob on his shoulder.

Kato noticed, for the first time, several official-looking vehicles parked around the estate, and dozens of men in various types of uniforms busy marking spots that looked like blood along the driveway that led directly to O.J.'s front door.

Neighbors were now beginning to gather outside his gates, trying to catch a glimpse of what was going on. Suddenly a Chevy Suburban appeared out of nowhere, came flying down Rockingham, hit one of the police vans, and clipped off its sideview mirror.

Several cops immediately waved it down, approached the driver, and angrily asked him what he thought he was doing. In the general confusion, no one was sure what to expect. The fellow turned out to be a neighbor whose only "crimes" were curiosity and bad driving.

A.C. then emerged from the house, with a child holding each of his hands, on his way to deliver them to Nicole's parents. Kato watched as Cowlings helped them into his White Bronco, one identical to O.J.'s, and drove away.

As Kato was about to be put into the backseat of the police car, David Horowitz, a local TV reporter pulled up. He happened to be one of O.J.'s neighbors, saw that something was going on, leaned out of his window, and asked one of the uniforms to fill him in.

As Kato was taken away he looked behind through the rear window of the police car at the opening moments of what was about to turn into one of the ugliest media circuses Los Angeles, or anywhere for that matter, had ever experienced.

On the ten-minute ride to the Bundy police station in West Los Angeles, the same precinct where the children had first been taken, one of the uniformed officers explained to Kato what to expect. He would not be left alone at any time. "Two detectives will meet you, take you upstairs, and ask some questions."

They pulled into the lot, and the two officers handed Kato over to a policewoman who introduced herself as Lisa Brickhouse and put a patch on Kato's shirt that read *visitor.* She led him inside and ordered him to sit by her desk. Someone then came by and reminded her that civilians weren't to be held in this area of the precinct, causing Kato to wonder if that meant he was, in fact, a suspect. Brickhouse then moved him to an area filled with snack-food vending machines and a couple of round tables. To Kato it looked less like an interrogation room than a place where officers went for short breaks. Because of the early hour, no one seemed quite sure what was going on, or what to do.

Brickhouse explained that two detectives were on their way to question him. She then asked if he wanted something to eat. "All we can offer you is prison food," she said without humor. Kato asked what they were serving.

"Burritos."

It was about 7:45 in the morning. Kato politely declined. Another officer volunteered to make a run to Del Taco, or anyplace else. Once again, Kato declined.

Two hours passed before the detectives who were scheduled to question him arrived. They met up with him in the "break" area, introduced themselves as Detectives Brian Carr and Paul Tippen, and ordered him to follow them.

They took Kato to a room on the second floor of the station, cold and bare except for a metal desk and three chairs, one on one side and two on the other. There was a single interior window with a venetian blind to prevent an unobstructed view of the rest of the floor.

He prepared himself to be questioned. Instead, the two detectives told him to take a seat, and left. The door automatically closed and locked behind them.

After a while Kato had to go to the bathroom. He tried the door and couldn't get it to open. He then tried to wave down a detective on the other side of the window, but was ignored by everyone. Eventually, someone did pass by and, without asking, seemed to know what he wanted. He took Kato to the men's room. On the way the fellow said, casually, "Hey, what do you know about all this mess? Pretty awful, huh?"

Kato was surprised by this sudden burst of casual chat. "Yeah, I guess," he said. As he stood by his stall another detective took the one next to him and said, "You're pretty good friends with O.J., huh?"

"Both of them," Kato said, meaning O.J. and Nicole, as yet unaware that there was a second victim. He was then taken back and locked again in the same room.

It wasn't until noon that Carr and Tippen returned. Now they wasted no time in getting down to business. The questions came fast and hard. Why didn't O.J. and Kato go to the McDonald's on Wilshire, which was much closer to Rockingham than the one on Santa Monica?

"I have no idea," Kato said.

"Are you sure?"

"I wasn't driving. I had invited myself along for dinner and hadn't asked where we were going."

The questions continued, over and over, as if Kato had not answered any of them. "Kato," one of the detectives said, "when you went for dinner with O.J., did you drive by Bundy?"

The detectives went over the details of that drive at least a dozen times. After a while Kato became convinced they were trying to trick him. "Through it all I kept thinking to myself, I wasn't supposed to go to McDonald's with O.J. . . . I wasn't supposed to go . . ."

After what seemed like hours to Kato, they moved on to another set of questions. When O.J. paid with the twenty-dollar bill, did Kato notice any cuts on his fingers?

He told them he hadn't. No cuts, no Band-Aids, nothing.

Eventually, they shifted back to the drive. Did O.J. drive by Bundy, past Nicole's house?

No. For the millionth time. Carr leaned in close and put his face right into Kato's. "Hey, man," he said softly, "if you're lying to us, you know you're going to jail." He paused. "Are you lying to us?"

Kato was visibly frightened. "No," he said in a tiny voice. "Guys, I've told you nothing but the truth. I haven't got anything to hide. I'm telling you everything I know."

Tippen then said, "We're trying to be your friend, here, Kato."

"I appreciate that."

The two detectives left the room again, and returned about a half hour later. They began the same questions over again. Kato would give the same answers, and this time, when either Carr or Tippen repeated them, they'd make small "mistakes," which Kato would correct. For instance, "Now, Kato, you said 475 Bundy," and Kato would say, "No, I said 875 Bundy." He was convinced now they were trying to trap him.

This continued until three o'clock. Kato had now been unofficially locked up for eight hours. He began to wonder if it wasn't a good idea for him to have a lawyer. He asked Lieutenant Carr if he could make a phone call. Carr said all right and led him down the hallway to a desk with a telephone.

Kato dialed his own number, to check his messages by remote code. He noticed how long it took for the tape to rewind. The first message was from his mother, in Milwaukee. She was crying. *"Kato, Kato, you're not dead . . . tell me you're not dead. . . ."*

He looked at the phone receiver, startled at what he'd heard. He had no idea what she was talking about. "Her message scared the shit out of me."

The next was from his actor friend and business associate Grant Cramer. "Kato," it began, "if you're there, man, pick up . . . this can't be true . . . you're not dead . . . you can't be dead . . ."

This was followed by a dozen messages from friends, all saying the same thing. "I began to freak. Why did everybody think I was dead?"

It wasn't until later in the day that he got an answer to that question. A reporter had leaked a story that there was a second victim, and that he was an actor. When Grant first heard the report over the radio, he immediately got into his car and drove to O.J.'s to see if Kato was all right. He put two and two together and came up with a dead friend.

When Cramer arrived at Rockingham, he was surrounded by reporters. He identified himself as Kato's friend and asked if there was any new information on the victim. From the physical description—young, tall, blond, handsome, and an actor—Grant concluded it was Kato. He told the press they had been friends for years. The reporters wanted to know the victim's name. Grant spelled it out for them K-A-T-O K-A-E-L-I-N.

Not long after, the news was being flashed around the country. A friend of Kato's mom heard it in her car radio and called to express her condolences. That's how his mother first heard the news. She in turn tried to call him and, when she could only get his machine, feared the worst and broke down crying.

After listening to the numbing messages, Kato put the phone down and, in a daze, followed Carr back to the interrogation room. He sat down and the two detectives once again left. Kato figured they were going to see if they had succeeded in tracing his call.

Another hour went by before they returned. "Now this is it, Kato," Carr said. "I'm going to ask you for the last time, did you lie to us? About anything? Because if so much as one thing you told us turns out not to be completely true, I promise you will go to prison for it."

"Guys," Kato said, whipped with exhaustion, having gotten no real sleep since Saturday night, "come on, I told you, I didn't lie . . . I told you nothing but the truth . . . I swear to God. . . . " He was near tears, but it didn't seem to matter to the detectives. They kept coming at him with the same questions over and over.

Kato began to beg to be left alone, and at one point asked if he could go home. To his utter surprise, they said fine, he was free. They even volunteered to drop him off.

A shaken Kato Kaelin asked to be taken back to Rockingham. Carr suggested it might be in his best interest if he didn't go back there right away, because the entire area had turned into a circus.

Kato asked to make another call. They brought him to the same phone and he called Cramer, who was shocked and relieved to hear his friend's voice. He told him to come right over. Carr and Tippen arranged for a black-and-white to take

Kato to Grant's house on Wilshire Boulevard, near UCLA, in the Westwood section of Los Angeles.

When they dropped him off, Kato got out of the car and was greeted by Grant and his girlfriend Kathy, outside the house. Grant threw his arms around Kato and hugged him tight. "Man, I'm so glad to see you! I thought you were dead! Everyone thinks you're dead!"

Kato now had the feeling he was being watched, either by the police or someone else. He was extremely jittery, scared and fatigued. It was in this state that he decided to confide in his friend.

Later on, when articles began appearing in the tabloids, with information only Grant could have known, and photos of Kato, Grant, and Nicole that Grant claimed were stolen, an infuriated Kato would deny the stories and suspect it was Grant who'd sold him out, for money.

Exhausted and depressed, Kato decided he needed to lie down.

After a fitful two-hour nap, Kato called O.J.'s house to see what was going on. He also needed some fresh clothes. Media circus or not, he knew he had to go back.

A cousin of O.J.'s, Terry Baker, answered the phone. They talked for a while, and as they did so, Kato turned on the TV. For the first time he got a sense of what was taking place at Rockingham. There were media trucks everywhere, surrounding the estate. Reporters, neighbors, passersby, "looky-loos," police. The entire neighborhood seemed packed with people. Kato decided to wait until dark before returning.

As night fell he asked his friend to drive him to O.J.'s. They both got into Grant's black Thunderbird and made their way back to the house. As Kato got out at the Rockingham gate and went to use his key, several police came over to find out who he was. He explained that he lived at the house, but was getting nowhere until Lisa Brickhouse, who happened to be there, told the others he was okay, and escorted him in.

TV cameras had by now formed a crush around him. The eleven o'clock news would lead with this footage and ask the question, *"Who is the mystery man behind the gates of the O.J. estate?"*

Inside, the house was packed, mostly with O.J.'s relatives, among them his sister Carmelita, O.J.'s mother, his sister Shirley, her husband Ben, their daughter Terry Baker (whom Kato had talked to on the phone earlier), Arnelle, Jason, Jason's girlfriend Jennifer, and several small children, sons, daughters, nieces, and nephews of the Simpson clan.

Howard Weitzman, the criminal attorney O.J. had first retained, was there, as was Leroy "Skip" Taft, O.J.'s business lawyer. Also present were Robert Kardashian, and A.C. Cowlings. Each came up and hugged Kato, telling him how happy they were to see him.

He went into the living room and felt as if he'd entered a scene out of some surreal movie. Ten feet in front of him O.J. sat in his big, beige easy chair directly opposite the projection TV. All Kato could see was the back of his head. Everyone in the room was focused on the screen as O.J. channel-surfed the continuous news coverage.

And the news wasn't good. "O.J. is going to be arrested—" *ZAP.* "O.J. Simpson has a mysterious cut on his index finger—" *ZAP.* "O.J. Simpson was taken away in handcuffs—" *ZAP.*

It was inescapable. Every station was following the breaking events, and all had come to the same conclusion. O.J. Simpson was suspected of murdering his wife. Kato: "I didn't see any emotion in him, and that bothered me. . . . I felt sick to my stomach." Each time a reporter said something O.J. didn't like or agree with, he would shake his head and say out loud, "That's not true! That's not true!" At one point a reporter came on and said O.J. couldn't account for his whereabouts during the time of the murder. Again he shouted, "That's not true," then added, "Kato knows where I was! *Kato knows he's my alibi!* Where's Kato?"

At that point, he turned, saw Kato in the house for the first time, smiled, pointed, and said, "Kato went to McDonald's with me."

"'Yeah, O.J.,'" Kato remembers saying out loud. "I was on the spot with everybody there and I didn't know what he meant by 'alibi.' Did he mean I went to McDonald's with him? 'Yeah,' I said, 'I did go to McDonald's with you.'"

"And Kato knows I went back in the house after."

According to Kato, "In my head I went, 'No, I never saw you go in the house after McDonald's.' And I didn't. The last thing I remembered seeing before going into my room was O.J. standing by the driver's side of his Bentley. But now I could feel everyone's face on me. I said nothing, but in my head I was screaming to myself, '*What am I doing here? What's going on . . . ?*' I was afraid for my life."

Before he could actually say any more, someone else angrily shouted at the TV in response to something else a reporter said. Kato felt relieved to have the pressure off him, even for a moment.

There was a constant stream of caterers from restaurants all over the neighborhood coming by and dropping off what seemed like tons of food, free of charge. Every minute another one came calling at the Ashford gate. Each time he was let in, a gang of reporters tried, without success, to gain entrance to the house.

117

As soon as the food hit the kitchen, waves of people would help themselves. It seemed to Kato "the whole place was turning into some kind of foodfest! I didn't get it. How could these people have any appetite for food at a time like this?"

Kato took a seat behind O.J. and watched the news along with everyone else. A commentator was saying that O.J. claimed he had cut his finger in Chicago. According to Kato, his eyes drifted down to O.J.'s left hand, and for the first time Kato noticed a piece of tissue wrapped around one of O.J.'s fingers, which O.J. clutched tightly. He could clearly see rich red blood from the deep and still unproperly treated wound seeping through. He thought back to the night before, when O.J. seemed so eager to help search for a "prowler" behind the house. The thumps. The weirdness that followed. And now this. He wasn't sure what to think and he began to feel sick to his stomach.

A few minutes later O.J. got up and went to the kitchen. He signaled for Kato to follow him. O.J. put a small plate of food together as Kato propped himself up on the sink area. O.J. said softly, "This sure is a mess."

"Yeah," Kato said.

"You know we went to McDonald's, don't you, Kato?"

"Sure. The police questioned me about that and I told them we went to McDonald's. They asked me if we drove past Nicole's house on Bundy and I said no."

"And when we came back I went into the house. . . . "

Kato felt the temperature fall in his mind. He said, "Yeah, I think . . . I don't really . . . I went in my room. . . . " O.J. looked at Kato for a second and didn't say anything. "I didn't feel any sense of remorse [on O.J.'s part] over what had happened to Nicole," Kato recalled. After what seemed like an eternity, O.J. left the room and returned to his chair to watch more news.

The man who had sent Kato to his room with nothing more than a stare had now tried to convince him he was his alibi. It was unbelievable and unnerving. It also went unmentioned throughout Kato's entire sworn testimony.

Friends of O.J.'s continued to stream in and join the group in the living room. Outside, the media kept their lights shining on the house. If anyone went to the shades to peek through, the lights would set the room white.

The crowd didn't start to thin until midnight. It was then that Kato first spotted Gigi, the maid. She was in one corner of the living room, crying, repeating over and over again how confused she was. Kato put his arm around her and assured her that everything was going to be all right.

Sleeping arrangements were made. Kato volunteered to camp in the living-room, near Gigi. He put a blanket down on the living room floor and tried, without success, to drop off.

Strange and awful noises kept him awake. At one point O.J.'s mother, who was not in good health, repeatedly had to go to the bathroom and vomit. Throughout the rest of the house, the inescapable sounds of frightened, crying children filled the night.

The next morning, Tuesday, June 14, 1995, breakfast came in the form of another in the seemingly endless, free deliveries from local food establishments. The delivery people had to fight their way through the media crush, thicker even than the day before. By early morning, Kato was up, dressed, and returning the dozens of phone calls left on his machine.

About two in the afternoon, he received a call from Robert Shapiro, who informed him that he, Shapiro, was taking over as O.J.'s criminal lawyer. This was at least two days before the official announcement would be made. Shapiro requested a private meeting that evening, between himself, Kato, and "Skip" Taft, O.J.'s business attorney, to be held at O.J.'s nearby office complex on San Vicente Drive. Kato agreed.

By this time, O.J. was no longer at Rockingham. At one point Monday night, he had snuck out of the house and relocated to Robert Kardashian's, where he would remain in seclusion the rest of the week.

How did he elude the press that night? There is a secret entrance and exit to the house that, to this day, very few people even know exists. A path near the pool, very close to the rear alley, leads through the tennis court to a neighbor's yard and driveway, from where anyone—a thief, a prowler, an accomplice, a legendary sport figure trying to escape the press—can walk out quietly from the Rockingham estate onto a deserted Brentwood street.

The large-screen TV, which had been on since the moment of O.J.'s return from Chicago, continued to play to whoever happened to be watching at any given time. Now, Kato noticed, the mix at O.J.'s had shifted considerably, with more faces he didn't recognize, and fewer he did. Most, he assumed, were friends of either O.J., Arnelle, or Jason, none of whom he had ever spent much time with before this week. Every so often someone would go over to either Arnelle or Jason and say, "How can they do this to your dad?" or "Look at what they're doing to O.J. . . . My God, what's wrong with them?"

Jermaine Jackson came by. So did Jonah Wilson, a relative of the Beach Boys, Dionne Warwick; the stream was endless. At one point, Mark Slotkin, a friend of O.J.'s who'd been married to Robin Greer, a friend of Nicole's, came by with Bobby Chandler, a player for the Bills when O.J. was the team's charismatic leader.

Bobby and Slotkin joined the others in the living room, forming a loose circle, and began to reminisce about the "good times" they'd all had when O.J. and Nicole were together. To Kato, the afternoon began to take on the ghoulish green edges of a wake.

Then, according to Kato, something "weird" happened. Mark Slotkin said out loud that he'd heard something that afternoon about "noises" outside Kato's room Sunday night. Kato wondered how he knew that. In fact, Kato thought, Slotkin seemed to know an awful lot, including the scheduled meeting that night with Shapiro. Suddenly Slotkin looked directly at Kato and said, "You better get your story straight, man. This is O.J. Think about what you know, and make sure you really know it."

My God, Kato thought. What was he talking about? And who was he, anyway? They'd met once or twice, and now here he was talking to him in a way that made him extremely nervous, and once again fearful. Kato got a crazy feeling that his own safety might actually be in some kind of jeopardy, and he needed to get away to somewhere he'd feel safer.

Arnelle and her boyfriend Jonah volunteered to drive Kato to O.J.'s office for the meeting. They left the house and were mobbed by reporters. Kato recalled later, "We barely got out in one piece."

When she dropped Kato off, Arnelle told him to call when he was finished and she'd pick him up. It began to feel as if everyone in O.J.'s camp was trying to make very sure Kato was never completely out of their sight.

Skip Taft was the first to greet Kato when he entered O.J.'s suite. He was ushered into a large office and for the first time introduced to a waiting Robert Shapiro, who thanked him for coming. "I understand what you must be going through," Shapiro said, and added, "I hope it's okay if I ask you a couple of questions."

"Fine," Kato said.

Shapiro turned on a small tape recorder and began a series of rudimentary questions; who was he, where was he born, where did he live, what did he do for a living? No problem there.

The next series focused on Kato's relationship with Nicole. How did he meet her, how long had he known her, how long had he lived at her house, had he ever seen her and O.J. fighting? These questions made Kato a bit uneasier.

Shapiro then focused on the events of the previous Sunday, the day of the murder. What happened when O.J. was getting ready to go to the dance recital? The trip to McDonald's? The thumps on the wall? The duffel bag? The alarm?

Throughout the interview, Shapiro's cellular phone kept ringing. Each time he'd excuse himself, talk into the receiver; and say things like, "We've got to find him, wherever he's at," and then return to the interview.

The next time it rang, Shapiro's face lit up. He'd found someone he'd been searching for, Michael Baden, the forensics expert. He'd been a little hard to locate, as he was away on vacation in Pennsylvania. Kato heard Shapiro tell Baden, " . . . we'll fly you out, you'll get here, we'll take care of all your expenses . . . " When he finished, he flipped the phone closed and said to Skip, "See how fast I can get anybody? Pretty good, huh?"

Skip said yes.

Another call came in, this one from Henry Lee, the blood expert. Then another, from F. Lee Bailey. Kato thought to himself, these are very powerful men coming together.

Then the regular office phone rang. It was O.J. Skip answered and Kato heard him say, "Yeah, O.J., Kato's here right now."

Shapiro asked Kato to leave the room for a few minutes. He sat in the secretary's area, just outside the main office, close enough to overhear Shapiro's part of the conversation. "Don't worry," he heard him say. "We've just acquired the services of Henry Lee . . . Yes, Kato is here . . . nice guy . . . "

The conversation ended and Skip fetched Kato to continue the interview.

At one point, Shapiro asked Kato how he was doing. Kato said fine, and said again that he would be totally honest about everything.

"That's all we want you to do, Kato. Just tell the truth."

When the interview concluded, Shapiro turned off the tape recorder. Kato asked him to tell O.J. that he loved him, missed him, and was praying for him. Shapiro then silently stared at Kato for a long time before speaking. When he did, his words were pointed. "Do you think he did it, Kato?"

Kato returned the stare. After a pause he said, "God, I hope not."

Later on, when I asked Kato if he thought Shapiro had formed an opinion and he said yes. It was Kato's feeling that on Tuesday night, June 14, Robert Shapiro thought O.J. Simpson was guilty.

(Months later, when Shapiro and Kato would again meet, at Shapiro's request and with Kato's attorneys present, prior to his testifying at length when called by the prosecution, Shapiro's advice would be quite specific. "Just say yes or no. I'm a very direct yes-or-no kind of guy. You do stuff like this [elaborate] and Ito will eat you alive.")

The interview had taken two hours. When it ended, Skip called Arnelle, who soon came by to return Kato to the Rockingham estate, for all intents and purposes now the O.J. "compound."

Back at the house, in the kitchen, Arnelle stuck by Kato

123

and at one point asked him how it had gone with the lawyer. Kato ran down the questions Shapiro had asked, and when he got to the thumps, said, "I noticed for the first time that Al Cowlings was standing behind her, staring at me with a look of disgust on his face. I smiled at him and nodded, but he didn't smile back. I wondered what that was all about. I felt sick to my stomach, even though I hadn't eaten in nearly two days. I couldn't understand why A.C. had looked at me like that. I hadn't done anything." Once again, fear crowded his confusion.

Arnelle and A.C. left the kitchen together. Kato stayed behind, wanting to be by himself for the first time, really, since the morning. "I had the feeling I was being watched, that anything I said and did was being monitored, evaluated. I suddenly felt the need to get out of there. I decided to call Grant and ask him if he minded picking me up and letting me stay at his house."

Grant said sure, and soon was outside the gate, waiting. Just before he left the house, Kato received a phone call from Howard Weitzman.

"Hey, Kato, how are you?"

He said he was doing as well as could be, under the circumstances.

"Hey, man, how's it going?" A chill caught Kato in the back. He knew that voice on the extension. It was O.J.

"'Juice,' I said. 'How are you? Is everything okay?'

"'Yeah,' he drawled. 'I'm okay.'

"'What can I do for you? Anything?'

"'Just tell the truth.'"

After a night of spotty, shallow sleep, Kato rose early and asked Grant to take him back to O.J.'s. It was the day of Nicole's wake and he needed to pick up a suit.

They arrived at O.J.'s by eight, and already the bathrooms were clogged with people trying to use the showers. Fortunately, Kato had already bathed at Grant's. He got to his room, rummaged through his clothes, and found a dark, clean and pressed suit hanging in the closet.

Outside, two limousines were waiting to take the family to the service. The night before, detailed plans had been drawn up as to who would ride with whom. Kato was penciled in to go with O.J.'s immediate family. However, five minutes before the limos were to leave, he received a phone call from Cathy Randa, O.J.'s administrative assistant.

Shirley, O.J.'s sister, said she would take it. She spoke to Cathy for a few minutes, then held the mouthpiece while she announced that there was no room for Kato in any of the family cars. Word had come down, from where she wouldn't say, that Kato had to find his own ride.

He was shaken by this, and asked Shirley if he could speak directly to Cathy. "Cathy," he said when Shirley handed him the receiver, "what's going on?"

"There's simply no room for you. The limos are strictly for family." Kato said, softly, that was fine, and hung up.

He walked out the front door and watched as everyone got into their designated cars. He noticed that friends of Jason and Arnelle were getting into the family limos. That's when he knew for certain that he was no longer welcome at the house.

Kato walked up to Terry Baker, O.J.'s cousin, and told her his car was parked outside the gate, but someone had set up a camera tripod on it, and people were sitting all over the hood.

Terry told him not even to try to get to it, that he could take her car. She handed him her keys and he thanked her. She was parked inside the gate, which made her car easier to get to. However, because all the cars were jammed together, he couldn't move it. As he tried to rock back and forth he heard voices behind him, shouting at Terry for lending him her car.

That was it. Kato turned the ignition off, got out, handed her back the keys, and decided to make a try for his own car after all.

He opened the gate and began to push his way through the crowd. A camera appeared out of nowhere and accidentally caught him on the right side of his face. He continued to plow on, until he reached his car. He got in and tried to kick the engine over, worried that because he hadn't driven it in five days it might not start. As he cranked the ignition a TV cameraman scurried to remove the tripod from the car's hood.

Kato kept stalling out of nervousness. Finally, after one of the limos cut something of a path through the media, Kato kicked in, pulled up behind, and followed it down Rockingham toward the 405, headed south.

By this time Kato was sweating profusely. "I couldn't understand why I had been dissed by the family. I was the same Kato I'd been before Sunday night. I hadn't done anything to anybody except tell the truth. I couldn't understand why I was being treated like this. I followed the limo down the freeway. In my rearview mirror I noticed a van following me. I figured no way, but sure enough it turned out to be a television crew trying to shoot some footage."

Kato's heart began to thump with the same kind of urgent pounding he'd heard outside his window the night of the murders.

The wake was held in Dana Point, at a funeral home about an hour south of Los Angeles, where Nicole's parents live. Kato arrived, parked his car, took a deep breath, and went inside. He was greeted first by Lou Brown, Nicole's father, who appeared to be holding up well. While he and Kato were talking, Robert Shapiro appeared and walked up to Mr. Brown to express his personal regrets.

Kato (like Nicole) had been born and raised Catholic, and had attended many wakes. This one, however, was different. He remembered the times he and Nicole had gone to church together, something they both loved to do early Sunday mornings.

There were several familiar faces in the growing crowd. There was Robert Kardashian, Nicole's sisters—Denise, Dominique, and Tanya—her step-brother, Maria, Nicole's housekeeper at Gretna Green (the first house she'd lived in after the divorce), and Maria's husband, Rolf Baur. Faye Resnick says she didn't attend the viewing because she was too upset. Cora Fischman says Resnick didn't make the viewing because she was having her hair done for the funeral. At one point, Rolf came up to Kato and said quietly that he was going to "murder the bastard that did this."

Dominique, in tears, came over to Kato. She wanted to warn him that Nicole, whose body was on view in the chapel, didn't look anything like her real self. "Kato," she said, "it's not her in there. Don't be shocked by what you see."

Kato braced himself and went in. He walked over to the pew beside the silk-lined, whitewashed pine casket and knelt. He steeled himself for the worst as he looked at Nicole . . . and was surprised to see how genuinely beautiful she seemed in death. She was dressed in a black blouse that completely covered her neck all the way up to her chin. Her hair was fluffed and her face meticulously made up. A large silver cross lay atop her chest.

Kato hung his head and prayed for her soul.

———

When he finished, he left the room and stood in the hallway by himself. Several people approached to ask how he was doing. He decided he preferred the solitude of the chapel, returned to take one last look at Nicole, and say good-bye.

There was a small settee at one end of the room, where O.J. was sitting. Kato hadn't noticed him the first time. O.J.'s face was covered by his large hands. As if on cue, he began to wail: *"I no longer have a wife! I'm left without a wife . . . there's no more Nicole . . . I don't have Nicole anymore. . . . "*

Kato: "For me, I thought it was possible he was crying crocodile tears. The impact of sadness on his part just wasn't there."

Kato decided he couldn't stay in there anymore. As he got up to leave, Cora Fischman, one of Nicole's neighbors and closest friends, came in. Of all Nicole's friends, she was the most obviously devastated by what had happened. Now she became hysterical. When she saw Kato, she cried at the top of her lungs, *"Kato . . . Nicole . . . She's gone . . . How could this happen?"*

Cora went up, threw her arms around Kato, hugged and held him tight. When she finally let go, she turned and saw O.J. She went to him and began to pound his chest. *"What? What happened? What about the kids?"*

O.J. cried, "I loved her too much!"

"Why did you do this? How could you? Why did you do this?" she said as she started pounding his chest.

"I'm sorry," O.J. said, "I'm sorry."

Kato backed out of the room to the hallway, telling himself none of this could possibly be real. He stood alone until Maria and Rolf came to comfort him and take him out of there. As he left the chapel he saw Robert Shapiro once again, conferring with Mr. Brown.

A reception was held at the Browns' home. Kato went for only a little while, then drove himself back to Los Angeles. It was then he decided he wasn't going to return to O.J.'s. He wouldn't "officially" move out, just never go back. Instead, he drove to the home of his friend Alan Mehrez, the producer of *Savate*.

When Kato arrived, Alan's wife, Deborah, made him something to eat, and afterward, feeling a little stronger, realized he'd have to return to O.J.'s one more time for the rest of his things.

When he pulled up to the gate and managed to fight his way through, he found his guest house filled with sleeping strangers. At that point, Kato found himself a corner in the living room of the main house, and quickly fell asleep.

He awoke the next morning, Thursday the sixteenth, and got ready for the funeral. The services were being held at St. Martin of Tours Catholic Church in Brentwood, on Sunset Boulevard. The celebrant was Reverend Monsignor Lawrence O'Leary.

Kato took a shower, dressed, and had coffee. He asked Susan Wilkinson, one of the Wilkinson sisters, if she would drive him to the church.

He was among the last to leave the house, and when he arrived, he found the church packed. He was immediately greeted by several familiar faces, including Faye Resnick, Cindy Garvey, Mark Slotkin, Bobby Chandler, Steve and Candice Garvey, Bruce Jenner, T. K. Carter, Robert Shapiro, Robin Greer, and Byron Allen. Marcus Allen, O.J.'s famous protégé, was noticeably absent from both the wake and the funeral.

A.C. Cowlings had put Simpson friend Ron Shipp, an ex–police officer, in charge of security. Cowlings was standing with Shipp when Kato arrived. "He's okay," Cowlings said to Shipp. "You can let him in." Kato noted to himself that this was the first time A.C. had seemed even halfway friendly since the night of the murders.

Kato went inside the church and took a seat on the far right-hand side, six pews from the front. Cici Shahian, one of Nicole's inner circle of friends, took the seat next to him.

The closed casket sat in the middle of the church. Juditha (Judi) Brown, Nicole's mother, gave the eulogy. The priest spoke, followed by Denise, and finally Dominique. Communion followed, after which everyone walked by the casket to pay their final respects.

At this point, things began to get a bit out of control. The line kept backing up with grieving, weeping friends and relatives. People stopped to hug one another in the aisle, which caused those standing behind to begin to gently push forward. The backup spilled onto the altar and into the private recesses of the church. The priest finally had to announce that if the line didn't move more quickly, he would have to halt the service.

O.J. sat through all of this in the front row, immovable, his eyes covered with dark glasses. Howard Weitzman came by and gave him a hug which seemed more like a tackle, shook him by the shoulders, and told him to be strong.

When Kato passed, he went to O.J. and said, "I love you."

"Sorry to put you through this, Kato," O.J. said. "Sorry to put you through this."

"I just want you to know I'll be there for you always, in any way I can."

Kato went outside and, although the parking lot was filled with people crying and hugging one another, he couldn't find a ride to the cemetery, which was back in Dana Point. Finally, Rolf offered him a seat in the family car. All during the ride,

Rolf seemed extremely angry, and kept on repeating how he hoped "whoever did this to Nicole rots in hell for all eternity."

The slow ride to Dana Point seemed to take forever. Once Kato arrived, he could see that the burial was a much smaller and more private gathering than the church services. It was an incredibly warm day, and several people appeared to be on the brink of heat stroke. The older ones were allowed to sit.

Beside Nicole's draped casket were photos of her in the Ferrari, with the kids sitting on the hood, all of them smiling and radiant. It was one of her favorite pictures. There were others on display as well, including several of Nicole taken at the house on Gretna Green.

After the services, Kato noticed, every one of the Browns made it a point to hug O.J.

There was one last reception at the Brown home. Several of Nicole's friends were present, including a fellow by the name of Dino Buccola. He was young, good-looking, and a friend of both O.J. and Nicole, and had dated Nicole's sister Denise for four years. Although they were no longer seeing one another, and though he wasn't the boy's father, he was continuing to help raise Denise's little boy, Sean.

At one point, Buccola asked Kato to come with him to the market to get some more soda and beer. Along the way he kept talking about how unbelievable it all was. Kato listened and said little. He really didn't know Dino, but was grateful that someone had felt comfortable enough to share their feelings with him.

Back at the house, Kato spent some time with Sydney and Justin. The two children seemed a bit confused by what was going on. There were helium balloons everywhere. Kato asked Justin to write a note to his mother and promised that when he finished, he, Kato, would send it to her.

Justin found a pencil and a piece of paper and wrote, "Mommy—I miss you, I know you're in heaven." Kato attached the note to the balloon and Justin became very excited as he watched until it completely disappeared into the high, clear sky.

Kato went back inside the Browns' home and spotted O.J. sitting alone on a sofa. He watched as Sydney and Justin went to their father. Kato got the uneasy feeling that this might very well be the last chance O.J. would have to be with his kids for a very long time.

Arnelle and Jason invited Kato to ride back with them to L.A. in their limo. Kato accepted the offer, hoping it meant he was back in the Simpsons' good graces.

Everyone seemed to be in an up, almost party mood, remembering stories and telling jokes about Nicole. Back at Rockingham, there was more food, more people, more memories. Everyone was there.

Except O.J. He was nowhere to be found.

Kato slept that night at Grant's house, hoping for a little relief from everything and everyone. As it happened, Grant's turned out to be not much of a refuge. For one thing, his girlfriend was living there, and both wanted to know every detail of what had taken place since the night of the murders. They kept trying to get information out of Kato. He kept on wanting them to shut up.

Grant persisted and kept talking about how much he'd been on television these last few days. At one point, he turned to Kato and said jokingly, "When they make the TV movie out of your life, they better call me!"

According to Kato, Grant kept talking about how much

money he'd already turned down to tell as much as he knew. He said he'd been offered upward of a hundred thousand dollars. Kato responded by saying he was grateful for his support and hoped Grant would allow him a little space.

As if that weren't enough, calls kept coming from well-meaning people warning Kato he ought to watch himself, that he was being followed, that his life was in danger. Security officers, friends of friends, people who either might have or should have known more or better, all felt they were "helping," but instead, Kato recalls, "they were scaring the shit out of me."

One such misguided person was actually a friend of Grant's, who'd come by the house that night and, after leaving, called to say he'd seen a suspicious-looking car outside.

Another time, Grant claimed he'd found a bucket outside one of his windows and next to it cigarette butts. The bucket, he concluded, had to have been left behind by someone trying to stand on it and spy through the window. Maybe taken some pictures. Maybe worse.

"I began to wonder," Kato recalled later. "Was I a target?"

Friday the seventeenth, the phone started ringing at six in the morning. Grant picked up the receiver. It was for Kato. Detectives Tippen and Carr were calling to say they were coming by to take him in for a little more questioning, and that he, Kato, should be ready to go by eight.

Kato immediately called Alan Mehrez.

"'Alan,' I said. 'Those two detectives want to talk to me again. Do you think you could represent me?' Alan had been a lawyer before he got into the film business."

"I'm not a criminal lawyer, which is what you need. You want me to see if I can get you one?"

Kato said that would be great, the only problem being that the detectives were on their way to pick him up as they spoke.

"Wait for me," Alan said. "If they get there before I do, don't say anything."

Alan arrived at Grant's house a little before eight. As it turned out, Carr and Tippen didn't show until 8:30. When they did, Alan introduced himself and was handed a subpoena. "What's that for?" he asked.

Carr said, directly to Kato, "You are required to appear before a grand jury today."

Fine, Kato said, except he had no idea what a grand jury was. He began to shake.

"This is ridiculous," Alan said. "He's supposed to testify before a grand jury today? He doesn't even have a lawyer. He has to have time to get one." He excused himself and called Paul Hoffman, a friend and criminal lawyer.

"We have to go," Carr said.

Kato turned to Alan. "What do I do?" Alan nodded for him to go with the detectives, and asked Tippen where they were taking him.

"Parker Center, downtown," Tippen replied. "His lawyer'll know where it is." With that, they put Kato in a car and drove off.

On the way, Carr took out a piece of paper and showed it to Kato. "This the statement you made on Monday? Read it over and see."

As he did, he noticed a number of small, but consistent errors. Among other things, they made the same mistake regarding the address of Nicole's place they had made during his interrogation. Kato pointed them out, and Carr said okay, he would see to it that the corrections were made.

Fine, Kato thought. But why were they there in the first place?

When they arrived at Parker Center, Kato was taken out of

the car and marched through a maze of cubicles to a holding room similar to the one in the station at West L.A. he'd spent so much of Monday in. Carr asked him if he wanted coffee. Kato said no.

He waited, alone again, for what seemed like an hour before Carr and Tippin returned and ordered Kato to follow them. They went down an elevator, through a parking garage and a series of what seemed like endless hallways. Kato no longer had any sense of where he was and began to worry that if Alan somehow did show up with a lawyer, they'd never find him in time.

He eventually ended up at the DA's office, was taken into a room, and introduced to David Conn, a Los Angeles DA, and Deputy District Attorney Marcia Clark.

Clark, dressed in a blue business suit, seemed, to Kato, quite friendly. *Too* friendly. Especially when she opened her eyes wide, put a big smile on her face, and said, "Hi, how you doing? Can I get you anything? We're going to have a great time!"

"I knew right then and there she was going to be trouble," he said. "She asked me to follow her. Once again, I was on the go. She took me to her office, which, I couldn't help noticing, had a large poster of Jim Morrison on one wall. When she saw me looking at it, she smiled and said, 'You like Jim Morrison? So do I.'

"She opened a drawer and took out a bag of buttered pretzels and offered me some. I shook my head no. She asked how I was. I said a little nervous and then she began."

"Are you a friend of O.J. Simpson's?"

"Yes."

"A friend of Nicole's as well?"

"Yes."

"Now," she said, "let me ask you some questions. You live in O.J.'s guest house, right?"

"Yes."

"A nice guest house?"

"Very nice."

"You have a bed?"

"Sure."

"By a back wall, right?"

Kato felt he was being treated like a preschooler, and wasn't going for it. "Would you mind if I waited for my lawyer?"

That's when Clark's demeanor took a sudden, radical shift. Her smile disappeared. Her eyes grew harder. "What are you hiding, Mr. Kaelin?"

Carr chimed in. "Yeah, Kato, what are you hiding? Come on, you can trust us."

"Jeez, you guys are trying to trick me. I want to wait for my lawyer."

"What are you hiding?" Marcia Clark said, louder this time.

"I've got nothing to hide! I'll talk to you! I'll tell me everything I know! I just want to wait for my lawyer!"

"Fine," Marcia Clark said, and continued. She went through the now familiar set of questions, beginning with the drive to McDonald's, whether or not Kato noticed a cut on O.J.'s finger (no), why O.J. took the route he did (didn't know), and then suddenly, she opened a new line of questioning. "Now, near your room, is there a pool?"

"Yes."

"A Jacuzzi, too?"

"Yes."

"How often do you swim there?"

"Not often. Once in a while."

"Are there rocks around it?"

"Yes."

"A dirt garden?"

"Can we please wait for my lawyer?"

"*What are you hiding?*"

"Nothing. You're trying to confuse me!"

"You have to take three steps down to your room?"

"Yes."

"There's a screen door?"

"Yes."

"What is next to your room?"

"Arnelle's room."

"No, no, isn't there a pool room?"

"Oh, yes."

"How big is it? Can you get into it from your room?"

"No."

"It's separate, right?"

"Yes."

"Is there a way to get behind it?"

"No."

"Are there things in it like gloves, things like that?"

"I don't know."

"Would there be a wooden stick in there?"

"Where?"

"The pool room."

"I'd like to wait for my lawyer."

"What are you hiding?"

"Yeah, Kato, what are you hiding?"

Endless questions. What was kept in the pool room? Did he ever notice a wooden stick, a spiky thing kept in there?

"Did you ever go in that room?"

"No."

"You've never been in that room before?"

"Maybe I opened the doors once, I know it's there, I know it's a pool room, I know the machines that keep the pool heated are in there, but—"

"Could anything be hidden in there?"

"I don't know."

"Can you get behind it?"

"God, I don't know. . . . "

"You want a pretzel?"

"What are you hiding? Come on."

"Mr. Kaelin," Marcia Clark finally said, leaning in and smiling, "are you having fun yet?"

He looked at her and said, "Hey, is there a two-drink minimum?" With that, the tension broke and everyone started, of all things, to laugh.

Just then a small, bald, bearded man Kato described as looking like the character actor and playwright Wallace Shawn, entered the room. He was accompanied by Alan Mehrez. Kato was never so happy to see anybody in his life. "Alan," he said, "I can't believe you found me."

The other fellow began to speak. "My name is Bill Genego and I'll be representing Mr. Kaelin." Alan had somehow come through. "My client will remain silent, and I'll answer any further questions for him."

Marcia Clark looked at her watch. "It's five to one. You can have three minutes with your client before we take him to the grand jury. He's scheduled to appear at one o'clock."

"That's ridiculous," Genego said. "How can you subpoena him for a grand jury the same day you want him to testify?"

Clark stared hard at Genego. "Mr. Kaelin is going to testify at one o'clock and that's that."

Kato had no idea what was going on. Genego turned to him and told him not to worry. He then asked for a room to consult with his client in private. David Conn offered his office.

Once they were alone, Genego turned to Kato and said calmly, "We're going to go down to the grand jury and ask for an intervention. That's a postponement. Trust me on this."

Kato looked at the fellow. Trust him? He'd never set eyes on him before in his life. He knew him for a total of one minute.

Clark knocked on the door and announced that it was time. As they all walked to the grand-jury room, she and Genego continued to be at each other's throats, arguing over whether or not Kato was actually going to get on the stand and testify.

Kato was put into another holding room, adjacent to the grand jury. Genego made one final attempt to reason with Clark. "Look," he said, "this is ridiculous. My client and I haven't had any time together. I haven't read the case. I don't know what the police know. I haven't even had a chance to look at their reports!"

"Fine," Clark said, and turned to Kato. "You're going to testify. That's it." She then turned back to Genego and added, "If you try to stop him, I'll have you arrested for obstruction of justice."

In response, Genego tore a piece of paper from a pad and wrote down all that he wanted Kato to say on the stand. It read: "On the advice of my attorney, I must respectfully decline to answer and assert my right to remain silent."

Kato read it as they went through a final set of doors and he found himself in a huge room that looked like nothing so much as a college lecture hall. About thirty people sat around the room in wooden rows.

He was led to a large wooden seat that resembled an electric chair, sworn in, sat down, and waited.

Marcia Clark wasted no time. "Mr. Kaelin, on the night of June 12 . . . "

"On the advice of my attorney, I must respectfully decline to answer and assert my right to remain silent."

This scene was repeated a half-dozen or so times. Kato sensed a great deal of sympathy for him, from everywhere except the district attorney's table. When it became apparent he wasn't going to cooperate, the foreman of the grand jury stood up, looked at Kato and said the following:

"Mr. Kaelin, I advise you that your refusal to answer the questions put before you is without legal cause and that if you persist in your refusal, you will be in contempt of this grand jury and I will order you remanded forthwith to Department 122 of the Superior Court for the County of Los Angeles for further proceedings regarding this contempt."

Kato had no idea what the foreman was talking about. It sounded like something out of an old *Dragnet* rerun on Nickelodeon. He was sure he was going to jail.

Kato turned to the judge and asked if he could consult with his attorney. Permission was granted, and in private, Genego advised Kato to maintain his silence and say nothing except what was on the note.

He retook the stand, and the foreman asked him one final time if he was going to cooperate. Kato read his statement again and at that point was declared by the foreman to be in contempt of the grand jury.

The foreman then ordered a sheriff to escort Kato to the Superior Court room down the hall for an immediate hearing on the contempt charge.

Kato gingerly stepped down from the witness stand, looking and feeling hopelessly lost. Genego told him this was what was supposed to happen and everything was going to be all right.

One of the major issues was whether, in fact, Kato could be granted immunity before the grand jury, which would then automatically remove his Fifth Amendment rights, designed to protect any witness from self-incrimination. Immunity removes that possibility. Once a witness is granted it, he or she is forced to answer any and all questions or face likely imprisonment.

At the Superior Court hearing, presided over by Judge Stephen Czuleger, Marcia Clark was asked by the court why she simply wouldn't grant Kato immunity.

She responded that it might taint Kato's value as a prosecution witness by suggesting that he, indeed, had something to hide, and the DA's office had been forced to "bargain" for his testimony. Besides, she added, Kato wasn't entitled to immunity because he had already told the police what they wanted to know.

Judge Czuleger pointed out that there were really two issues involved, one having to do with the Fifth Amendment, the other with the Sixth—a person's right to counsel. "If a person wants to confer with his lawyer," the judge pointed out, "he's entitled to do so. Especially if he's a witness and not a defendant." This, of course, was at the heart of the dispute. Clark's office had treated Kato in every way as a suspect and defendant, falling just short of charging him in the case. There were just too many unanswered questions.

Clark told the judge that since Kato had been taken into custody that morning, he was, in fact, a defendant, and therefore the Sixth Amendment, and possibly the Fifth, no longer applied.

The judge replied that no warrant had been issued for Kato's arrest, and that according to the records, he hadn't been handcuffed when taken to the station, so technically speaking, he wasn't a defendant at all. At best, the judge said, and this might be stretching it, he was a suspect in a murder case. Most likely, he was a witness, albeit an important one. The judge asked Clark what the downside was to giving Kato a weekend to consult with his lawyer and properly prepare for testimony, "putting aside he may flee the country and be in Brazil by morning."

Everybody in the courtroom laughed.

In reality, Clark was not trying to avoid giving Kato a chance to get together with Genego—as it had become fairly apparent to the district attorney's office that Kato was not going to be charged with any crime—but an opportunity for the defense team to talk to him before he testified. What she didn't know at this point was that Kato had already met with Shapiro earlier in the week, at O.J.'s office.

Czuleger turned to Kato. "Trust me. Don't go anywhere. You wouldn't like the alternative. Be here Monday at 8:30 in the morning."

As soon as the judge hit the gavel, he was handed a piece of paper by the bailiff. He paused and then announced to everyone in the courtroom that O.J. Simpson was now officially a fugitive from justice.

No one had known during the hearing that the infamous Bronco chase was in full progress and being televised live across the nation and around the world. O.J. Simpson was no longer a mere suspect, or one more fugitive trying to slip into obscurity to escape the long arm of the law. He was now the most famous fugitive on the planet!

Kato and Genego walked out of the courtroom and into a scene out of a thirties movie. They were spared the waiting crush of reporters only because they were all busy rushing down the hall shouting into their cellular phones that "O.J. was on the loose!"

Kato arrived back at Alan's house a little after three, and watched the rest of the Bronco "chase" on TV. There was a Knicks play-off game scheduled for that evening, to be broadcast from the East Coast, which Kato had originally planned to spend the evening watching. Now, as the chase dragged into the darkness of night, the game was reduced to one corner of the screen, with no sound. The rest of that station, and all the channels, were filled with live coverage of what was rapidly becoming known everywhere as "the crime of the century."

Kato watched, along with the rest of the world, as A.C. Cowlings and O.J. arrived back at the house. He could clearly see Jason, Arnelle, and several other familiar faces in the landscape of the TV screen. He could also see the snipers set in the trees, their rifles aimed at the Bronco sitting outside the front door of O.J.'s main house. He watched as Jason broke loose from the pack and ran toward the car, only to be pushed away by A.C. And he watched as, finally, a weary, defeated O.J. got out of the white vehicle and quietly surrendered to the waiting detectives.

What followed was a rebroadcast of Robert Kardashian's earlier reading of O.J.'s "suicide note," which Kato now saw for the first time. He watched, grimly fascinated, as Kardashian stood before a phalanx of microphones and read from O.J.'s handwritten note.

To Kato it *sounded* like a suicide note, but he wasn't going for it. He felt it was nothing more than a scam, that O.J. wasn't going to kill himself. None of it rang true. As for Paula, that was all wrong too. A lie. That wasn't how O.J. felt. He'd told Kato on numerous occasions he didn't love Paula and would never marry her. So what was he talking about?

However, the notation at the bottom was what really did it. There, on TV, was a close-up of a "smiley face" O.J. had drawn in the O of his signature. "I love O.J., but in my gut I was worried that either O.J.'s people or the Brown family, or anyone, might think I was taking sides. And I had heard things, the result of which, the bottom line, I was afraid for my life."

Kato began to realize who his friends were, who he could depend upon and who he couldn't. Alan Mehrez offered him a place to stay as long as he felt he needed it. That night, he began to make arrangements to pick up his things from the guest house. Each time he called, however, he got a member of the family, or the defense team, and was told that they "weren't ready" for him to come by. A month would pass before he would be allowed to return to the house and get his things.

When he was finally given the go-ahead, Kato called two of his best friends, Tom O'Brien and Will Stumpe, and asked if they would give him a hand. They all arrived at Rockingham, and Kato found his belongings piled up in the garage—at least what was left of them. He discovered that there was a lot missing, including photographs of him with Nicole and the kids, his phone message tapes, boots, several pairs of shoes, shirts, jackets, and various other items personal in nature and of value only to him. He would never get any of them back. The few pieces of clothing that were left behind, mostly jeans, had their pockets turned inside out, as if they had been searched.

They left the house and noticed a van following them. They cut into a Shakey's pizza parking lot. The van pulled up and rolled down its window. The three held their breath, not knowing what to expect. A voice from inside the van yelled out, wanting to know if there was a news story here.

Throughout the night, each time he heard a car pass, he'd wait for an accompanying knock on the door. He didn't get much sleep and it wasn't until morning flooded the room with sunlight that he began to feel a little better. Being at Alan's was a big help. A real family seemed a welcome relief.

But the good feeling didn't last very long. That morning's newspaper screamed headlines about "A Secret Witness" who had sought immunity before testifying.

Wrong, Kato thought. He had been willing to testify. He only wanted a little time to prepare with his new attorney.

All day TV and radio reports kept asking, "Who is this secret witness and what has he got to hide?" After breakfast,

Kato and Alan watched the continuous news coverage until he couldn't watch anymore.

He had arranged to meet with Bill for most of the day. Genego had volunteered to represent Kato gratis, a gesture Kato greatly appreciated, especially with a bank account hovering precariously close to zero.

Kato arrived at Genego's office by early Saturday afternoon and the two were soon deep into the nuts and bolts of their approach to the upcoming testimony.

At first, Kato was slightly uneasy, feeling that Genego suspected he might actually have had something to do with the murders. Every so often Genego would look at him in a strange way, or so he thought, until he realized this came with the territory, and he was doing what he was supposed to.

They met for several hours, interrupted by a rash of phone calls, including a couple from Robert Shapiro's office, seeking another meeting, and one from Carr and Tippin, who said they wanted to ask Kato a few more questions. Genego told Kato "it was very smart to play both sides."

That afternoon, Kato told Genego everything he knew and afterward, Genego explained what to expect from the grand jury.

For the rest of the weekend Kato kept a low profile, catching up on sleep at Alan's and waiting, as if on death row, for Monday morning's inevitable arrival.

On June 20, shortly after eight o'clock, about a half hour before his scheduled testimony, David Conn and Marcia Clark escorted Kato to a private room. He could tell immediately their attitude had undergone a major shift. They now appeared genuinely friendly and polite to both him and Genego. Since

O.J.'s arrest, immunity was no longer an issue. Kato didn't seek it, Clark didn't offer it. Instead, they talked about what she intended to ask him on the stand.

Under oath, Kato was examined by Clark, who led him through a series of questions regarding his relationship with Nicole, how they'd met, when he moved into her house, how long he'd lived there, when he moved to O.J.'s. She then focused on the events of Sunday, June 12.

It was a long and difficult examination. It lasted more than two hours, and at its completion, Kato was dismissed.

It didn't take very long for the press to identify Kato as the mysterious "secret witness." That same day, his face was, for the first time, plastered across the front page of every newspaper in the country. All the TV stations, which continued to cover the story on an around-the-clock basis, began to make inquiries about Kato's identity, and his connection to the case. Kato began to worry that O.J.'s people would somehow come to believe all this meant he was conspiring against The Juice.

Kato also wondered what the Brown family must be making of all of that had taken place, especially this past weekend.

And Ron Goldman's family as well.

Early the next week, the grand jury was suddenly and unexpectedly dissolved. A grand jury is convened for the purpose of investigating whether or not there is sufficient evidence to charge a suspect with a crime. Witnesses are called and evidence is put forth. As no suspect is as yet formally charged, no defense arguments are presented.

The key to a grand jury is confidentiality. All testimony, and information relating to any investigations and testimony, must be kept from the public and, therefore, the jury. If this rule is somehow violated, the grand jury loses its power to effectively indict. As it turned out, just such an event happened, at least according to Judge Czuleger, when Robert Shapiro successfully argued that the jury had been "tainted" by the unprecedented public interest in and media attention to the case.

But there may, in fact, have been another motive for the dismissal of the grand jury. A rumor traveled through the DA's office that the court was leaning toward an indictment only for manslaughter, *if that,* and in order to save its "murder one" case, the DA's office had pressured the grand jury to dissolve before any indictments were handed down.

Either way, once the grand jury was dissolved, District Attorney Gil Garcetti called for a public preliminary hearing. California is one of the states that give an unusual chance to the government to seek an indictment against a suspect. Still, it is unusual for The People to pursue any sort of case when it fails at the initial grand-jury stage. Garcetti, however, feeling the pressure from several high-profile cases in which the district attorney's office looked less than effective in the court of public opinion— including the extraordinary acquittal of the officers involved in the Rodney King beating (some were later found guilty on federal charges), and the mind-boggling hung jury in the Menendez brothers' trial—was not about to lose the O.J. case with the whole world watching, before he even had a chance to try it.

Garcetti announced that his office was going forward with a preliminary hearing, and Kato was among the first witnesses to be formally subpoenaed. This meant he would have to go through the whole process all over again, and this time in full view of the public. Worse, it was almost certain to be televised live.

———

Before actually testifying, Kato spent a lot of time going over the events.

"I couldn't get Nicole's face out of my mind. I'd close my eyes and see her—so vibrant, beautiful, and alive. Then I'd see her lying in her casket, dead.

"I was afraid. After my appearance before the grand jury, everyone, from my lawyer to the detectives who gave me a ride back to Alan's house that day, advised me to keep a low profile. I began to wonder why." Yet again, the fear returned. "Was I in some kind of danger?"

He spent his nights tossing and turning in bed. He lost his appetite. He tried to run ten miles a day but discovered he didn't have the energy. He wound up spending most of his day the way everyone else did. Watching "The O.J. Show" on TV.

He spent a lot of time on the phone talking to Rachel. Stories kept appearing about them in the press, making them into an "item," which they weren't, although they did spend some time together after the murders.

Kato kept seeing people on TV and in the tabloids who claimed to be "close friends." A fellow he hardly knew was featured on a local news program insisting to be his best friend.

He was now in the grip of an out-of-control media, feeling the squeeze ever tighter around his neck.

Early on the morning of Tuesday, July 5, Kato arrived at the courthouse. A few days before, two detectives he hadn't dealt with before called Genego and suggested that they all meet the day of Kato's scheduled testimony at a "secret" location; from there they would personally escort him into the court building, thereby avoiding the press. The clandestine spot turned out to be nothing less than a Mexican restaurant in downtown L.A. where a lot of the detectives, including several associated with the case, hung out. Genego and Kato met the officers there, got into a car, and were driven through a side entrance of the courthouse.

Once the detectives parked, they escorted Genego and Kato to a holding room. En route they passed the open door of Gil Garcetti's office. Kato looked in and saw the unsmiling face of the DA, who returned his look before slamming the door in his face.

In the holding room, Kato was greeted by Detective Vannatter, who was also scheduled to testify, and several members of the Brown family.

As the time grew nearer for Kato to be called to the stand, he came down with a bad case of nerves. Patty Jo Fairbanks, Marcia Clark's assistant, noticed his agitation and asked if there was anything she could do. Kato asked if it would be all right to call his mother in Milwaukee.

Patty said she would arrange it. She took Kato into her office, dialed his mother's number, and let him have a few moments of privacy . . . the last he would get before the world would overwhelm him.

Detective Vannatter testified immediately before Kato. Now that Kato was no longer under suspicion, Vannatter's attitude toward him changed. He was much friendlier now. Kato began to look upon the detective as a kindly grandfather type; previously he'd thought of him as the no-nonsense slightly constipated-looking detective he'd encountered those first awful hours.

When Vannatter finished his testimony, he returned to the holding room, where, along with Genego, he resumed watching the proceedings on TV. Genego complimented the detective on his grace under pressure. "I can tell you've done this kind of thing before," he said, smiling.

"Really? I was good?" Vannatter then turned to Kato. "You're an actor, right?"

"Yes," Kato said, surprised at the question.

"Well," Vannatter said, "I guess you guys sometimes work the same crazy kind of hours we do. I regularly put in seventeen-hour days, you know." He then began rambling about some of the more celebrated cases he'd worked on. "The Manson case," he said, "now there was a real biggie."

Shortly before it was Kato's turn to testify, Patty Jo took him aside and offered one last piece of advice. She told him not to worry about the effect of his testimony. "Anybody who's really your friend today will still be there a year from now."

Kato suddenly flashed on something he'd heard, that Jason had recently changed the name of Nicole's dog from Kato, which the kids had called it, to Satchmo, an act meant to convey the fact that he was out of favor with the family.

Marcia Clark appeared at this juncture in order to go over her questions. After this, Kato was taken out of the holding area and brought to yet another room, where he would remain for two more hours with Genego, who left him alone several times to use a pay phone in the hallway.

Kato noticed two large poster boards sticking out from behind a file cabinet. He pulled them out and looked at them. They were filled with photos of Ron Goldman's bloody body taken at the scene of the crime.

After getting over the initial revulsion, he began to wonder if they had been left there on purpose, for him to see before testifying. He got sick to his stomach.

———

It was 10:30 A.M. before he took the stand. The detectives who had driven him to the courthouse now returned to escort him to the courtroom. They walked through the final set of doors and what seemed like another mile to the witness chair.

He held up his hand and looked at Marcia Clark. She informed him that he was facing in the wrong direction. "That way," she said, indicating he should turn toward the bailiff. A slight ripple of laughter spread through the court.

For the next hour and a half, until the lunch break, Kato answered Clark's questions, mostly concerning the events of Sunday, June 12. The first time she asked him if he knew who Nicole Simpson was, she showed him a photograph, and left it in front of him the entire time he was on the stand. She knew it would be impossible for Kato to take his eyes off that photo, to forget, even for a second, that Nicole was no longer alive.

At one point during his testimony, he looked over to O.J. and the two made eye contact. It was the first time Kato had laid eyes on him since the funeral. He smiled, trying to let The Juice know how sorry he was for all that had happened. O.J. gave a slight nod, as if to say he understood, and that it was okay.

During her questioning, Marcia Clark kept on referring to O.J. as "the defendant," while Kato kept responding with "O.J." It became a little side game between the two, until Shapiro officially objected to her use of the term defendant. Clark responded, "Well, is he the defendant or isn't he?" Shapiro was overruled.

When the court adjourned for lunch, Kato was brought back to the second holding room by Patty Jo. While he was there, Denise Brown sent him a message. Her family wanted to see him.

Kato was escorted back to the first holding room, where the Browns and the Goldman family were. "Kato," Denise said, coming up to him, "you looked so nervous up there." He shook his head as everyone came over, took his hand and hugged him. He had never met any of the Goldmans before. Denise introduced him to them except for Ron's father, who was not present at that moment. They seemed genuine and warm, and thanked Kato for testifying.

He excused himself to go to the men's room and found Mr. Goldman there. They stood by adjacent stalls. Once more Kato started to feel sick to his stomach. He asked Mr. Goldman if he felt the same way. Ron's father looked at him, tried to smile, and said, "Take it easy, Kato." He washed his hands in silence and left.

That was the last time Kato saw any of the Browns or Goldmans outside a courtroom.

At the end of his first day of testimony, on the way to the holding room, Kato stopped at the water fountain. Three office girls quickly came over and asked for his autograph. He agreed, and before he had finished, he was barraged by the press. *"Hey, smile, Kato . . . hey, Kato . . . Kato, give us a smile . . . "*

It had begun.

He decided to cool out that night with a couple of friends at the Moustache Café in West Hollywood. As it happened, the table across from his was filled with reporters. Someone tipped Kato off that one of them was from a local TV station and had just called for a news crew to rush over. He was able to get out just in time. His nights of cooling out were over.

Back at Alan's, the phone kept ringing. Friends, reporters, lawyers, a steady stream of the familiar and the strange all tried to find him.

His second day, he took the stand after waiting four hours in the second holding room. A delay during the proceedings—no one could find the coroner—threatened to consume the rest of the day. Genego was convinced Kato was not going to be called that day, and he asked his client if it was all right for him to leave. Kato said sure, as long as he didn't have to testify.

"It won't happen," Genego said.

Kato was now alone in the second holding room. To break up the boredom, he decided to go down the hall and use the pay phone. He called a friend, and at one point during the conversation was told that a reporter on TV was saying he, Kato, was missing. He hung up and ran back to the holding room. There, a much-relieved Patty Jo led him by the hand to the courtroom.

Kato found himself back on the witness stand, with no lawyer present, about to resume his testimony before the entire world.

When he finished, the detectives took him to the elevator and down to the garage. On the way, one of them turned and told him to be careful. Kato asked about what and was told of the likelihood that he would be receiving death threats. He then handed Kato a card with a twenty-four-hour number on it. He was told that in the event of any direct threats being made, he was to call it immediately. "Don't worry," the detective reassured him. "Nothing usually comes of them."

In the garage, Kato was introduced to a new driver. He hadn't seen this one's face before, and was, by now, more than a little wary of anyone he didn't recognize being allowed to get so close.

As they left the courthouse the driver asked where Kato wanted to be taken. Wilshire Boulevard, he said, near Beverly Hills. He didn't want the driver to have Alan's exact address.

During the ride, they talked about, of all things, school. The driver said he'd gone to Marquette. Milwaukee, Kato thought to himself. His hometown. "Marquette basketball," he said. "I love it."

"Well," the driver said, "every Wednesday at six o'clock A.M., Mark Fuhrman, me, and a couple of the other guys play a little basketball. After this whole thing is wrapped up, you ought to come on down and play with us." He paused and then added, "And it won't be very long before it's over. You won't believe how much shit we have on O.J. that hasn't come out yet."

Kato got out of the car on Wilshire, not sure what had just happened. One thing he was certain of, he had no intention of ever shooting hoops with these boys.

At Alan's, there was a message to call his ex-wife. He phoned immediately. She told him she had heard on the news that local gangs loyal to O.J. were making death threats against Kato. They had publicly vowed to kill anyone who testified against The Juice.

By the end of the day, what one newspaper had already described as "the Kato Phenomenon" had taken firm hold. The next morning, dozens of offers from the tabloids started pouring into Alan's office. The TV tabs in particular were frantically outbidding each other for his story. At one point, according to Kato, *The National Enquirer* offered $350,000 for an exclusive interview. *Hard Copy* and *A Current Affair* were calling every hour, upping the ante to outbid each other, begging for an exclusive interview.

Alan decided to take Kato out for dinner that night. They drove to an expensive Japanese restaurant in Beverly Hills.

They didn't have reservations, but Alan hoped that because it was a weeknight, they might get lucky and not have to wait too long before getting a table.

Alan pulled his car up to the entrance, got out, and walked in with Kato. The hostess took one look at the two and said, very excitedly, "Oh, Mr. Kato, we have table for you right now!"

While staying at Alan's, Kato decided to go running every morning along Pico Boulevard. Whenever he did, horns would go off as cars passed. People would stick their heads out and call, *"Kato . . . Kato . . . Hey . . . Kato . . . We love you, Kato. . . ."*

Girls would drive by, pull over, take off their shirts, and give them to him. One girl handed him a "Free O.J." T-shirt.

The newspaper coverage was relentless. One fantastic headline screamed, KATO KAELIN NOW MORE RECOGNIZABLE THAN AL GORE!

One magazine headlined that the fifth-most-popular new name for babies was Kato. "Of course there was a part of me that enjoyed it," he said. "I'd be lying if I said I didn't. I was, after all, an actor, and had been in Los Angeles for nearly fifteen years trying to make a breakthrough. Now, finally, people were beginning to discover there was a guy named Kato Kaelin."

Not all the attention was positive. Scenes from movies and TV shows he had appeared in began to show up on tabloid shows. Geraldo Rivera broadcast a report on his TV show that Kato used drugs and dealt drugs. In Milwaukee, his mother was deluged by reporters and photographers. His brothers and sisters were suddenly being covered by the national press. At times they were threatened with "exposure." "We've got stuff on you we'll use unless you cooperate," they told his brother.

Everywhere Kato went, people asked him for his autograph.

The supermarket, coffee shops, bars, dance clubs. He couldn't take ten steps without someone shoving a piece of paper in his face and wanting him to sign it. People would come up to him and ask, "Who did it, Kato? Who did it?" Or, "Come on, man, free O.J. . . ."

Once, Genego received a call from someone identifying himself as O.J.'s "private investigator" and saying he was trying to find Kato. Genego said he was his lawyer and would take a message. According to Kato, the investigator said his message came directly from O.J.: "Kato, don't you remember me walking into the house after McDonald's?"

Recalls Kato, "The message did what I was sure whomever was really behind it intended for it to do. Scared the shit out of me."

One night, at the Coronet Bar in Beverly Hills, amid a crowd of "admirers," someone snuck up to Kato and whispered in his ear, "You motherfucker, I want to kill you!"

Photographers and reporters continued to follow him wherever he went. Celebrities invited him to private parties. He began to glimpse, firsthand that seemingly invisible Hollywood society of the rich and famous that coexists alongside the rest of the populace. Now, suddenly, after nearly fifteen years, through the most bizarre and unfortunate set of circumstances, Kato Kaelin had finally found himself in the spotlight. His picture made the cover of *People* magazine twice. He was named as one of the most "interesting" people of the year by *Time* and *Newsweek*. He hosted the *Talk Soup* cable-TV show.

In spite of his avowed silence, he announced through a press statement issued from Michael Plotkin's office:

As a result of the public's interest in all the matters surrounding this case, I have been flooded with requests for interviews and offered substantial amounts for my story.

I've never found it hard to speak from the heart and with truth. . . . I am deeply grateful for all your attention. I feel your concern. Please understand mine.

Not long after, he sold an "exclusive" interview to one of the TV tabloids for $50,000 . . .

. . . While O.J. Simpson, the man who had made Kato famous, sat alone in a jail cell awaiting trial for the murders of Nicole Brown Simpson and Ron Goldman.

3

Life Before the Simpsons

Who is Brian "Kato" Kaelin?

How did he come to live with both the victim and the alleged murderer of the so-called crime of the century? What makes him such a fascinating, if not compelling, figure in the case? Is he a joke? The ultimate Hollywood boy toy? A prime example of how to get by on fading good looks and no rent?

Or is he something else, a cold, calculating opportunist willing to drive his car over the bones of the dead in order to enter the temple of fame and fortune? This is the story of an utterly unremarkable life and the path that led it to the spotlight, the story of the Brian "Kato" Kaelin everyone thinks he (and especially she) knows.

He was born thirty-six years ago, March 9, 1959, in Milwaukee, Wisconsin, the next to youngest of six children. He has three brothers, John, Mark, and Bob, and two sisters, Gail and Mary. A fourth brother died at birth in 1967.

He first got the nickname Kato from the TV series *The Green Hornet,* which all the brothers watched as children. Kato was the Green Hornet's expert karate sidekick. For a while all the boys in the family were called Kato. Their parents were forever saying, "You Katos! Stop fighting!" The nickname stuck to Brian in high school, when he pitched for the baseball team. After that, no one who knew him ever called him Brian again.

His father was, by all accounts, a very warm and humorous man. He passed away in 1990 at the age of sixty-five from a heart attack. He was a diabetic, and eventually his love of the good life, eating the wrong foods, and maybe having a little too much to drink at the end of the day, finally caught up with him. He owned one of those cask-and-cleaver-type steak houses, and was also a sales representative for a major liquor distributorship. He did fairly well, as one might expect, since Milwaukee's major industry is the production and distribution of hard liquor. Some might say consumption of it as well.

By Kato's account, his was a typically happy, middle-class family. Money never seemed to be a problem. The Kaelins lived in a comfortable home in Glendale, right outside of Milwaukee.

Kato remembers laughing an awful lot as a child. He claims to have been blessed with a set of parents who had great senses of humor and got a big charge out of having a house full of happy kids.

Kato attended Our Lady of Good Hope parochial school. He was always the class clown. Because of his ability to make everyone laugh, including the nuns, he was able to get away with a lot more than most kids.

He stayed at Our Lady of Good Hope for eight years, until he entered Nicolet, one of the more affluent public high schools in Glendale. Eighty percent of the student body was Jewish. This was a big change for Kato and, in retrospect, probably a good one, for it helped this Middle American, somewhat sheltered boy realize the entire world wasn't composed of Catholics.

By now, it was clear to Kato that he enjoyed having an audience. He sometimes wondered why he had to stay in school at all, when all he really wanted to do was to entertain people, an ability he seemed to posess from an early age.

Kato developed into a fairly good athlete and in his freshman year made the baseball varsity team. This was a big deal at Nicolet, one of the very few times a frosh had done so. He was also good enough to earn the quarterback position on the freshman football team, before going on to JV. He started for the varsity team in his senior year and still holds the school's passing percentage record.

He also managed to find time to appear in as many school variety shows as possible and MC'd several of them, along with schoolmates Tom O'Brien and Will Stumpe, who are still his friends. O'Brien, whom Kato called the night of June 12, is a district attorney in Los Angeles. He and Kato go all the way back to grade school.

Will came into Kato's life in high school. He, too, now lives in L.A. and owns a highly successful lighting business.

Together, the three wrote their own material, and soon decided that even though they were underage, they were good enough to get work in local nightclubs.

Tom and Will were a year ahead of Kato. When they graduated, he became a solo act, and wound up writing and appearing by himself in the big spring variety show. He was also in the usual roster of classic high-school musicals, including *Oklahoma* and *Carousel*. Among his more wacky accomplishments was being chosen senior prom king.

After graduating, Kato enrolled in the University of Wisconsin–Eau Claire. He attended classes for two years, during which time he became increasingly involved in the communications department. He developed a weekly variety show on the school's cable TV called *Kato and Friends*, and a radio show as well. He was doing a lot of what today might be called "edge" comedy. Kato recalled making fun of a dean one time and having his show canceled. The next day, a petition appeared with three-thousand names, and it was promptly reinstated.

Kato also discovered girls in college, and when he did, determined to make up for lost time. He used to go from dormitory to dormitory in search of his next great conquest. In his freshman year Kato developed mononucleosis, the so-called kissing disease, which, being a good Catholic, he took as a direct Warning from Above. "That's when I decided that no matter what, I would not actually sleep with a girl until I got married, and that was one promise I kept. I stayed a virgin until, at the age of twenty-three, I met the woman who was to become my wife."

In 1979, during the spring break of his sophomore year, he decided to move to California. Tim Ryder, a school buddy, told Kato he and his parents were flying to Redlands, California, and knowing Kato was anxious to see the West Coast, he invited him to go along.

Kato fell in love with California the moment he touched down. Redlands is about eighty miles southeast of Los Angeles. Kato took one look at its gorgeous mountains and knew this was where he wanted to be. He suggested to Tim that at their first opportunity they relocate permanently, and he agreed. They returned to Wisconsin for the rest of the school year, then drove back to Redlands. It was the summer of 1979, then, when Kato made his first real pilgrimage west, with $900 in cash to his name.

Life in Southern California is a series of lessons learned, until one day everything changes and L.A. becomes a place where lessons are taught. It didn't take long before Kato learned his first, having to do with the lay of the land. He had no idea when he first moved there how far Redlands actually was from Los Angeles, which had been his real target. He was determined to pursue comedy as a career, and knew that Hollywood was where the action was. As he soon discovered, there weren't a lot of job opportunities in his chosen field in Redlands.

The pickings were so slim that his first actual comedy gig was as a busboy at a local restaurant called Edward's Mansion, a family establishment that offered live novelty entertainment along with the salad bar. Tim got a job there as well. Before long they were able to talk the owner into letting them do a little comedy during dinner hour. They worked every spare minute preparing for their professional showbiz debut, and on opening night laid a major bomb. Their big career move turned out to be the chance to advance from busboys to waiters. They grabbed it.

Kato and Tim had made a pact to stay in Redlands for a full year without returning to Milwaukee, no matter what. The plan was to establish full-time residency in California and become eligible for state school tuition benefits. They both wanted to complete their college educations, either at Cal State San Bernardino or Redlands, a college Kato favored because of its baseball team. In the back of his mind he thought if his comedy career didn't work out, he might take a stab at professional baseball.

Exactly one year to the day after they arrived in California, Kato and Tim enrolled at Cal State Fullerton in Orange County, near Yorba Linda, about forty-five minutes out of Los Angeles. They finally settled on Fullerton because in addition to having a strong athletic program, it was closer to L.A. than the other two schools.

Their major problem was not a unique one. Early on, Kato discovered a method to get by on very little money and lots of charm. He and Tim were almost broke. They put what little money they did have into a joint account. A big mistake. No matter how much either put into the account, there never seemed any funds to withdraw.

With no money, they had a little trouble getting a place to live. They finally did scrape together enough to rent a small guest house that belonged to an elderly couple. The only problem was that they didn't have a bathroom.

It was, however, perfect for the two boys. They figured out other ways to stay clean. Sometimes they used the bathroom of the house of the family they were renting from. When that wasn't available, they'd go to the nearby fraternity house, tell the residents they were thinking of pledging, and while they were there, take showers.

They became so popular at one house, SAE (Sigma Alpha Epsilon), that they did in fact wind up pledging. It didn't take long for Kato to become social chairman of the fraternity.

To pay their rent, Kato and Tim got jobs in a small pub just off campus, where they continued to develop their comedy routines. They were still struggling financially, when one of the women in charge of the school cafeteria, Mary Zahnzinger, felt sorry for them and, to keep the two from starving, passed the boys the nightly leftovers.

During the day, Kato would attend classes, mostly in advertising, which he had declared as his major, and at night perform with Tim. That is, until Tim met a girl and decided to move in with her, which effectively broke up the act. He eventually got married and moved back to Milwaukee, where he took a job working for his father's decidedly noncomedic steel business.

On his own now, Kato started driving down to Los Angeles

every weekend, looking to break into the comedy club circuit. Places like the Comedy Store and the Improv had an open-mike policy on Sunday nights where anyone could get up and try a few minutes of comedy.

"Although I had high hopes, this quickly became a lonely and depressing period of time for me. Often, I'd arrive at a club six o'clock on a Sunday evening and join the lineup for a chance to get on stage by 2:00 A.M., in front of maybe three people I'd wind up buying breakfast for after the show. I got absolutely nowhere at an incredibly slow pace."

After about a year of this, Kato stopped making a reverse weekend commute and concentrated all his efforts on finishing school.

He stayed at Cal State Fullerton for another two years, but never earned his degree, remaining to this day eight credits short. Even though he'd put in more than enough hours, he kept cutting back on class time. His interest in show business wouldn't go away. In his senior year, he took a job working as a comedian/waiter at a place called Bobby McGee's in Brea, near Fullerton. It was the hot hangout spot for all the college kids, and Kato made out "like a bandit," usually able to clear a hundred dollars a night, great money for him at the time.

"My routine went something like this. I'd go over to a table of customers, introduce myself, and say, 'Hi, our special tonight is lobster tails. Fifty cents apiece.'

"'Really?'

"'Sure. Once upon a time there was this lobster. . . . '

"That sort of thing. The restaurant was a theme place, so the waiters had to dress as various fairy-tale characters. It was fun, especially when large parties were booked. The management's policy toward what we could say and do was anything goes as long as we kept on serving food."

He worked at Bobby McGee's for two years, and became so

good at what he did that he was often sent to other franchises to help break in new staff.

It was during this period that Kato met a beautiful twenty-three-year old California girl, an aspiring model by the name of Cyndi Coulter. She had come into the restaurant to apply for a job as a waitress.

She got the job and they started dating. At the same time she began getting a lot of modeling work. For a while, *Playboy* was interested in having her appear in an aerobic-exercise video they were putting together, but nothing came of it. She was also interested in cosmetology, and wanted to enroll in a private school to get her license.

Kato and Cyndi fell in love and decided to get married. She was the first woman Kato actually made love to.

His family flew out from Wisconsin for the wedding. The night before, Kato got into an argument with his dad when Kato told him he thought he was making a big mistake, that he didn't want to get married after all. Mr. Kaelin told him he was just being nervous, the whole family was there, he had to go through with it, and everything would be fine.

Kato took his advice and settled in to married life. At first things went extremely well. He was making a lot of money at Bobby McGee's, and she was getting modeling gigs and starting to get noticed. They decided to move to Burbank, a suburb only minutes from all the Hollywood nightclubs and film studios. Kato was able to transfer to a local Bobby McGee's.

He felt ready to take another shot at "big-time" show business. They found a small apartment right behind the Walt Disney Studios, and Kato began taking acting lessons while Cyndi took a job as a cocktail waitress. It didn't take long for this lifestyle to create an impossible situation. As Kato remembers, "In spite of all our tender pledges to each other, and the birth of our beautiful little girl, Tiffany, we grew apart. We decided to split up after two years, and for the sake of our child, swore we would remain friends forever, which we have. So far. Still, I took the breakup really hard."

So did Kato's father. It was the first time in the history of the Catholic Kaelins that a member of the family had gotten divorced. For a while his dad blamed himself, believing he had pushed Kato into the marriage. Kato tried his best to convince his father that it wasn't his fault. He then tried to get Kato to pursue an annulment, which he didn't.

Looking back, Kato realized he never should have married in the first place. "I was only twenty-three years old, looked like I was twelve—and most of the time acted like it—had no career to speak of, no permanent place to live, and no real prospects. I was a tender babe in a very prickly woods."

The first thing Kato had to do was find a new apartment. He eventually moved in with two guys and two girls in a big house in Eagle Rock, near Pasadena. No one was coupled off, just five people sharing a place to live, like *Melrose Place* before it existed.

He still had his job at the Burbank Bobby McGee's and was working his tail off. Whenever he had any free time, he pursued acting work, and had the usual run of an aspiring actor's luck. None. He'd get cast in a major commercial the residuals from which would have amounted to enough to live on for a year, only to see his "big scene" wind up on the cutting-room floor. That kind of thing happened a lot. Each time, he'd grit his teeth and try to move on, believing that one day he'd turn a corner and things would start happening.

Kato continued to wait on tables for the next couple of years and, whenever possible, look for acting work. Time was always at a premium, and he'd come up with ways to get through such hour killers as rush-hour traffic jams. He had a fake head in his car, a mannequin he called "Doris," that would allow him to drive in the car-pool lane. He went so far as to make a special harness for it so it could move back and forth.

He tried every trick in the book to get himself hired. He'd take his picture, wrap it in clear plastic, and put it on the bottom of a pizza. He would then "borrow" a uniform from one of the many pizza delivery chains, buy a pie, and deliver it to a casting company. When he'd show up and they'd say they didn't order anything, he'd tell them the pizza was free, all part of a special promotion. He'd leave, knowing that as they reached for the slices the photo of his face would gradually appear, over which he'd scribbled, "The pizza is on me!—a joke, get it? I can be there for an interview in thirty minutes!"

People were always curious about the guy who'd dreamed that scheme up. It cost him about fifty bucks a week in pizza, but did manage to get him some jobs. He even landed a TV pilot out of it. Which, unfortunately, went nowhere.

After a while he got the opportunity to move back to his old apartment in Burbank. Cyndi, of course, was long gone. Kato took in a roommate, a fellow by the name of Arnie Krause, a very funny actor who became a good buddy. They got along well, and because each wanted to be an actor, were always rehearsing each other for auditions.

In 1987, Kato landed the lead in a low-budget comedy feature called *Beach Fever*. It went directly to cable and video.

Kato became friendly with the film's director, Alexander Tabrizi, one of those Hollywood personalities who always has a deal brewing, and is always promising someone a role in his "next big feature."

Kato followed up *Beach Fever* with a couple more parts in low-budget features, including a little horror film called *Lycanthrope*, a title that was changed to *Night Shadow* for video.

He also took an industrial show out on the road for Nissan, a corporate comedy convention-floor thing, which turned out to be a great gig. He teamed with a fellow by the name of Reno Goodale, who taught him a lot about comedy. Together they traveled across the country, made terrific money, and worked with dozens of beautiful models. The job was to entertain people who stopped by the Nissan exhibit at various car shows and get them to sit in a new Nissan. It was a lot of fun, and paid enough for Kato to rent a nice little place in Hermosa Beach, just south of Los Angeles.

Late in 1991, the twisting slowness of Kato's fate began to gain speed when Tabrizi called him to say he was producing a new film called *Little Red Corvette,* and while there wasn't a part in it for him, he wanted to know if he'd be interested in helping cast it. Tabrizi arranged for Kato to team up with another actor, a fellow by the name of Grant Cramer, who had recently completed a stint on the soap opera *The Young and the Restless.*

Grant and Kato met, hit it off, and together started reading actors and actresses for Tabrizi's film, which never got made.

One evening over dinner, Kato and Grant began to discuss exactly what it was they were doing. Tabrizi had asked them to "help out," which meant in the jargon of Hollywood that they *might* get paid *if* the film were made. Now that the project had fallen through, Kato and Grant decided that the casting business might be an easy and fun way to make some money for themselves. In June of 1992, they formed an "extras" company.

"We called ourselves the Performing Artists Group and worked out of Grant's apartment in Westwood. For a while we did really well. We got a lot of films to cast, and made more than enough to pay our start-up costs and expenses. Plus, we cast ourselves in all the films. It was a great way to meet a lot of new people and learn about the business end of the film industry."

Grant had an actress friend, Kim Dawson, who told the two about a film she was up for called *Surf, Sand and Sex.* Kato decided to audition for it and was offered a role. According to Kato, it was only *after* he accepted the job that he was told there was some nudity, which, although the camera seems to suggest otherwise, he steadfastly maintains he absolutely refused to do.

"I guess they really wanted me, or else couldn't find anyone else to play the part, but they were willing to compromise, and I wound up shooting this one particular scene wearing skin-colored briefs. I was supposed to be a mechanic who helps a woman after her car breaks down, and somehow they manage to have a romantic interlude." Nothing serious, nothing very naughty, but one day it would come back to haunt him. Rumors persist that he was a soft-core "porno" star. In truth, the film had less sex in it than an episode of *NYPD Blue.*

(Not long after he testified at the preliminary hearing, Barbara Bare, a porno star, gave an interview to a major newspaper that got picked up by the wire services, about what a great guy Kato was, and how much fun he was to work with. Kato claims never to have met or even heard of her.)

The casting business lasted for a while, until both Kato and Grant realized they were never going to make a decent living from it. Plus, Kato wanted to get more involved in producing. He had, by now, met and begun working for Alan Mehrez and his sister Diane's film production company, DEM Productions.

In 1992, Kato and Grant dissolved their partnership and gave their client roster to another casting company, in return for which they were to receive a percentage of whatever business they generated. According to Kato, their clients got a lot of work, but he and Grant never got their commissions. Looking back, the Performing Artists Group provided Kato with a lot of good times, if not a whole lot of money, unfortunately an all-too-typical Hollywood story.

However, it provided something that would prove much more valuable, for it established his relationship with Grant Cramer, and it was through Grant that Kato first met Nicole Simpson.

It happened in 1992, during Christmas week, a traditionally slow time in the film business. Grant suggested they go to Aspen for the holidays. Kato was a little concerned about the expense, but Grant assured him it wouldn't cost them all that much. They could drive, and he had arranged for a place to stay. Grant knew a lot of actors and actresses from his soap-opera days. One of them, a girl named Lynn, had a house in Aspen and had invited Grant and Kato to share it with her for the holidays.

They left Los Angeles Christmas morning and drove straight through to Aspen. No sooner did they unload their things than they hit the slopes. Grant was a terrific skier, Kato a novice. Fortunately for him, they weren't there primarily to ski. The real action at Aspen happens at the numerous nighttime parties.

"Every evening we were invited to or crashed a different one," Kato said. On December 30, they invited themselves to a celebrity bash at the Ritz Carlton.

"It was a very exclusive affair, filled with the upper echelon of Aspen players—movie stars, producers, directors, the Donald Trumps, and other regular members of the rich-and-famous cast. Grant and I decided to sneak in through the kitchen. We got dressed in our best clothes and simply rode up with the waiters in the service elevator. Nothing to it, really.

Once in the main room, they fanned out and began to mingle. "We were into talking to as many great-looking women as possible," Kato said. At one point, Grant saw someone he thought he knew. It was Nicole Brown Simpson. Grant had been introduced to her at a party at O.J. Simpson's house a while back. As soon as he saw her, he went for it. He told Kato he had "always wanted to do her." He tapped Kato on the shoulder and said, "Come on."

They went over, said hello, Grant introduced Kato to Nicole. It was obvious that although Grant thought he knew her, neither she nor the friend she was with, Faye Resnick, remembered ever having met him before. It didn't matter, though, for within minutes, they were all laughing together as if they were old friends.

At the time Nicole and Resnick were staying at the home of Jerry Ginsburg, who owned a condo in Aspen. An acquaintance of both Nicole's and Faye's from New York, Ginsburg had given the two an open invitation to use his place whenever they wanted. Jerry liked having beautiful women around, and a free place in Aspen was as good a way as any to accomplish that goal. As Kato was to find out later, O.J. hated Ginsburg. One time he'd come to L.A. and stayed at Nicole's place for a week. When O.J. found out, he went crazy. He and Nicole got into a big fight, with O.J. accusing her of bringing "that guy" into the house where his kids slept.

As far as Nicole was concerned, she liked Ginsburg as a friend and therefore saw nothing wrong with having him stay with her. She wasn't romantically involved with him, and he always slept in the guest bedroom. Still, in matters like these, there was no reasoning with O.J., and he never let up on Nicole about her friendship with Ginsburg.

In Aspen, the four got along well. Grant and Nicole had really hit it off. "I could tell there were sparks flying," Kato said. "I liked Faye, but only as a friend. I was really more interested in Catherine Oxenberg, an actress I had recognized as soon as I walked in. I excused myself and went over to talk to her. We struck a harmonious chord, and I wound up spending the night with her, while Grant returned to Jerry's condo with Nicole and Faye."

For the next several days Nicole, Faye, Grant, and Kato hung together, skiing, going to parties, and having fun. They passed their afternoons on the slopes, where Kato, as always, covered his lack of know-how, by playing the clown, falling down and making a fool of himself for a laugh. Their evenings would always begin with drinks at Jerry's condo.

At one point during the trip, Grant told Kato that he especially liked the fact that Nicole had recently gotten breast implants, which, he said, made her look even better than when they'd first met. Although Kato wanted to spend more time with Oxenberg, as a favor to Grant, who wanted some private time with Nicole, he agreed to spend some time with Resnick.

Nicole had just broken up with a fellow she had been seeing for a while, a young, Los Angeles–based law student. She'd enjoyed his company, but backed off when she started to feel he liked her a little too much and had become a bit smothering. He was after a "relationship," while Nicole was only looking for a good time. Her divorce from O.J. had just become final that fall, and she wasn't ready for anything permanent.

Quite the contrary. She was enjoying her newfound status as a "free woman." And she loved to party. Every day while she was in Aspen, this fellow kept calling her from L.A. She got his messages but never returned them. Once she met Grant, she told Resnick she liked him a lot, and the other fellow was "history."

They all attended a big New Year's Eve bash, which, by midnight, turned into a festive free-for-all, with everybody

175

kissing and hugging. The party began at someone's house, then moved on to the club Tatou. Afterward, Grant brought Nicole to the place where he was staying. Kato gave up his bedroom privileges so Grant and Nicole could be alone. He didn't see them again until the next afternoon, when they emerged from the bedroom and Nicole left for Jerry's condo.

Grant told Kato, although they'd done a lot of "fooling around," he still hadn't actually made love to Nicole. It was Nicole's choice, he said. She wanted to get to know him a little bit more before they actually "did it." This, according to Kato, only made Grant more determined.

They all spent the next day together skiing, and then hung out at a place called Schlomo's. There, someone snapped a photo of Kato hugging Nicole, which would appear in *Star* magazine after she was murdered. It was this photo that would feed the rumors that Nicole and Kato had been lovers. The truth is, although she would confess later to having other ideas, Kato and Nicole were never romantically involved.

On January 2, 1993, Kato and Grant drove back to Los Angeles. Nicole and Faye thought about accompanying them, but at the last minute decided not to.

Back in L.A., Grant continued seeing Nicole. A couple of weeks later she invited him and Kato to an engagement party she was throwing for her friend and, briefly, lover, Keith Zlomsowitch, at the rented house she had just moved into on Gretna Green Way.

Keith was the maître d' at the Mezzaluna restaurant in Beverly Hills, a favorite hangout of Nicole's. At this time Keith and Nicole were not romantically involved. Nicole's attention was entirely focused on Grant.

"One thing I remember," Kato recounted, "was that people kept on 'going upstairs' during the party. I asked someone what was going on, and was told that that was where everyone was doing coke. I do remember Nicole repeatedly going up and down the stairs. However, I never went up there, I didn't actually see anybody take anything harder than a drink."

Nicole seemed to love the fact that she was finally really on her own, and had spent lavishly on this first big party. She was totally in charge. There was lots to drink, great food, champagne, expensive caviar, all the good things. A lot of the friends she'd made while married to O.J. showed up, including Marcus Allen and A.C. Cowlings.

After showing Kato the downstairs, she took him out back, where the pool was, and the guest house. "God, Nicole," he said, "who lives here?"

"No one," she said.

"I'm all the way down in Hermosa. Boy, I'd love to move up to this part of town."

"Fine. You can have it," she said. Just like that. She made up her mind right then and there, which of course Kato appreciated, but didn't quite understand. After all, they hardly knew each other. Kato, believing this was, in his words, "a great opportunity," at first couldn't believe she was serious, and told her so.

She assured him she was. She insisted they take a closer look at the guest house. They walked in and he could see the place was already completely furnished. "You'll have to move all this stuff yourself, if you don't want it," she said.

"No problem," he said. "What are you asking?"

"Nothing. Don't worry about the rent," she said. "We'll work something out."

"I mean it. I really want to move here."

"Okay."

Kato spent that night at Nicole's house, as did Grant, who claimed to have finally made love to Nicole. Kato slept downstairs in the maid's bedroom. The next morning he was awakened by the sound of his name being shouted. Grant was

177

calling him from her room. He grabbed a cup of coffee and went upstairs. Nicole was nowhere in sight, but Grant was standing on the balcony, stark naked, looking very proud of his achievement.

Months later this scene would reverberate uneasily in the recesses of Kato's memory, when Nicole first told him that Grant was probably videotaped that morning by one of O.J.'s spies.

The next day Kato began to move his things into Nicole Simpson's guest house.

4

Life with Nicole

Marcia Clark: When you went to that Gretna Green house to the party given by Nicole Brown, did you notice that guest house in the rear of the property?

Brian "Kato" Kaelin: Yes, I did.

Marcia Clark: Can you tell us whether you had a discussion with her about that guest house in the rear?

Brian "Kato" Kaelin: I did.

Marcia Clark: What was the nature of it, of your discussion?

Brian "Kato" Kaelin: I said, "Nicole, who lives back there?" And she said, "No one." And then I said, "Could I?" And she said, "Well, if you do, you have to clean it out." And I said, "Great."

Brian "Kato" Kaelin lived in

the guest quarters at Nicole Simpson's rented house on Gretna Green Way, in Brentwood, from January 1993 until January 1994, when she decided to buy a condo on nearby Bundy Drive. At that time, although she wanted Kato to continue living with her and the kids and move to her new place, he decided instead to move into O.J. Simpson's estate on Rockingham.

By the second week of January 1993, Kato had finished moving into Nicole's guest house. It had taken numerous trips to move his things up from Hermosa Beach, as all he had to transport them was his small sports car. Still, he owned little besides his clothes, a few pieces of basic furniture, and a TV.

At nightfall on his first day at Nicole's, he decided to knock on her door and give her a progress report on his move. He hadn't as yet seen her that day. When Maria, Nicole's housekeeper, opened the French doors at the side of the house, he smiled and said, "Hi, I'm Kato, I'm moving into the guest house. You don't know me, so don't let the sight of some strange guy roaming the property scare you."

Just then, Sydney peeked out from behind Maria. "Who are you?" she asked, with an odd look on her face.

Kato grinned, put on a funny voice, and said, "I weel be your new nayborrr!"

She broke into a big smile.

"What ees your name, yong lahdee?"

"Sydney," she said, and added that it was okay with her if he moved in.

From that very first day Kato loved being at Gretna Green. The guest house was perfect for him, a large loftlike space, complete with its own bathroom. It had no kitchen. However, Nicole had given him a key to the main house and said that anytime he wanted to use it, including the kitchen, he should feel free. Because it was on the ground level and her bedroom was upstairs, she said he would able to come and go without disturbing her, the kids, or any guests, at any hour of the night or day.

The guest house was completely separate from the main residence. The entrance led to a pathway on the other side of the pool down to the front gate. That meant that he could come and go without disturbing anyone in the main house. If Nicole wasn't in the backyard or on her terrace, she would never see him, or even be aware of his presence. As far as Nicole was concerned, it was nobody's business, especially hers, who came to visit him or stayed the night.

As it happened, Kato saw Nicole almost every day, and quickly came to enjoy the sweet easy feeling that emanated from her house. She seemed completely at ease with having him there.

From his guest quarters, Kato could plainly see the back entrance of the main house. On the second floor, Nicole's bedroom had a balcony that overlooked the pool and faced the hills. She used to stand on it and lean over the railing, holding a lit cigarette, her blond hair glistening in the brilliant sunlight.

As Kato would remember, "She always looked so beautiful. When she'd see me, she'd get all excited and yell my name. 'Kato! What's up?' she'd shout. 'What's doing?' She'd always have music blasting throughout her house. There was one song in particular she loved more than any other, 'If You Lied to Me,' by Charles and Eddy. She played the CD every day, over and over. 'If You Lied to Me' was also her getting-dressed song, her psych-up song when she went out for the evening. These days, whenever I hear it, no matter where I am, I always think of her."

Brentwood is one of Los Angeles's fabled "show business" neighborhoods, where legends of the industry, past and present, mingle in a countrylike atmosphere. Quite a step up from the glamorous grunge of Hermosa Beach. To be sure, Kato had loved living in Hermosa, with gorgeous young women forever parading in bikinis on their way to the store for a carton of milk, and music blasting out of everyone's apartment from sunup to sundown. It had been great fun, but, in truth, not all that conducive to work. He was in his thirties now, and his days as a young leading man were definitely numbered.

He had, in the months prior to the trip to Aspen, spent more and more time in and around Hollywood looking for acting work, and the hour-long commute had become exhausting. For a number of reasons, some immediately obvious, others that would take a while to surface, the opportunity to move in with Nicole could not have come at a better time.

Their friendship had literally begun on a high note, in the mountains of Aspen, and, with his moving in, seemed about to deepen, until something happened Kato felt certain would result in Nicole asking him to move out. Not long after Kato settled in, her relationship with Grant came to an abrupt and ugly end.

It had been obvious to Kato, and to everyone else, that Nicole liked Grant, and that Grant liked her as well, but not with the same intensity. She wanted to have a real relationship with him, one that wasn't only sexual, and had let him know it.

Unfortunately for her, Grant wasn't in it for anything but sex. And now that he'd accomplished this goal, he seemed ready to move on. For Grant, at least this time, the hunt would prove better than the kill. Kato had no problem with how his friend felt. After all, he reasoned, it wasn't Grant's fault he didn't like Nicole the way she wanted him to. It was the way he felt. Nor was it Nicole's fault for having fallen so hard. Unfortunately, she got caught on the wrong end of the romantic stick and, as a result, got hurt. Nobody's fault really, Kato believed, just the way these things worked.

He was, however, aware of how upset Nicole was. As her relationship with Grant disintegrated, rather than letting it go, Kato watched her become increasingly obsessive. She'd quiz him every day about Grant. How did he spend his day, what were his nights like, what did he do with his weekends and with whom?

She told Kato she thought Grant was a perfect physical specimen, exactly her type. Kato thought he might do Nicole a favor and told Grant that she was crazy about him. Grant sighed and said, "God, I know, she's really into me, but I'm not into her, not like that. . . . " With good reason. What Grant hadn't told Nicole, or Kato, was that even before Aspen, he had met another girl, Kathy, and had decided to pursue a serious relationship with her.

Things worsened between Grant and Nicole during the Super Bowl. O.J. had been invited to be guest of honor that year and toss the coin at the opening ceremonies. The game was being played in New Orleans, and O.J. had invited Nicole to accompany him. Even though they were divorced, he still wanted, indeed *expected,* her to join him for all his important business trips. Sometimes she went, sometimes she didn't. This time she had agreed to go, became all excited about it, as did he, and then, at the last minute, changed her mind. O.J. was furious.

Grant invited Kato to a party to watch the game, and Kato asked Nicole if she wanted to come along. It apparently never occurred to him that Kathy's presence might create a problem. Sure enough, when Nicole showed up, she became annoyed when Grant paid more attention to Kathy than to her. Nicole became quite uncomfortable, and when she and Kato got home, she said she wanted to talk to him about what had happened.

It was the beginning of a new phase in their relationship, one in which Nicole would confide her innermost secrets to her new houseguest. That night she told him that for the first time in her life, being at the party had made her feel self-conscious about her age. After all, she told Kato, she was in her early thirties, and Grant's girlfriend was only nineteen, twenty tops. Nicole said she felt like she was not only the other woman in Grant's life, but the *older* woman.

Kato told Nicole he didn't think Grant would ever have become serious about her whether Kathy was in the picture or not. Nicole nodded in agreement, realizing that nothing more than sex was ever going to happen between her and Grant.

What she did next surprised Kato. She took a deep breath, straightened herself up, and in a tone of voice he hadn't heard from her before laid down one of the few ironclad rules she would ever issue. At no time, she said, was Grant ever to set foot on her property. He was not to visit Kato at the guest house, use the pool, or even enter the driveway. *Ever.*

That was, initially, a difficult thing for Kato to deal with, as his days were still mostly filled with trying to get acting work and running whatever was left of the casting business with Grant. Besides, they were really good friends.

Kato looked at the floor and said softly, "I guess that means you'll want me out as well."

"No, no," Nicole said, waving her hands in front of her. "You can stay. I want you to stay. I just don't want to ever see Grant again, that's all." Kato told her he would respect her wishes, and did. Eventually, Nicole and Grant came to an understanding of sorts and developed a decent, if distant, friendship.

At one point Grant introduced her to a group-therapy workshop run by Karl Wolf that he had started going to himself. Grant thought it would be good for her, and at his prompting, she attended a few sessions, which she later described to Kato as pop-psych social gatherings where everyone got together and talked about their problems. She quickly lost interest and stopped going.

It was typical of Nicole to feel the need to keep things bottled up inside until she could stand it no longer and explode. During such periods of emotional incubation, she would wave off confrontation, or give in to what the other person wanted. Both Grant and Kato thought that talking about her problems in front of a group might help her deal with them in a more constructive fashion. Kato especially had seen her pattern of behavior firsthand, in the way Nicole dealt with O.J. Even though they were no longer married, he was constantly trying to run her show, and to a large extent, she let him. In retrospect it probably seemed easier to her than actually trying to stand up to him and say no. And probably a lot safer.

In a way, Nicole's breakup with Grant actually brought Kato and her closer together. By talking through her situation with him, she realized he was someone to whom she could reveal her innermost feelings *without fear of recrimination.* Kato was certainly no rocket scientist, no substitute for any kind of legitimate therapy, and in all fairness he never pretended to be. However, for the year Kato lived with her, he became the one male in her life she felt she could be totally honest with. She felt she could tell him anything, no matter how personal or private.

She trusted Kato never to use anything she told him in confidence against her. She believed that he wouldn't, for example, listen to her all night and then run to Grant the next morning to tell him everything she said. As a result, the bond of friendship between them grew stronger.

"There's a saying that goes, 'Idle time is the devil's handiwork,'" Kato said. "That pretty much sums up my impression of how Nicole lived on a day-to-day basis. She seemed to have too much time on her hands and not enough to do."

Kato noticed that no matter how late she'd been up the night before partying, she'd always be up the next morning, in time to make the kids breakfast and take them to school. When she returned, she'd spend the rest of the morning sitting in the sun by the pool, her eyes protected by dark Ray-bans. She liked to wear a black tank top that showed off her excellent muscle tone—even more remarkable because she almost never worked out—and enjoy a cup of hot, fresh coffee.

Occasionally, on warm sunny days, Nicole liked to lay out topless, wearing only a thong on her lower body while she soaked up the sun. She had recently gotten breast implants, and "was proud and eager to show them off to me, if I cared to check them out. . . . I have to say that most of the time, life at Nicole's was really easy, although this one thing she did made me a little uncomfortable, especially since she'd keep turning herself over to get an even tan. She might be lying on her back, I'd pass, and suddenly she'd turn and there they were. It didn't take long for Nicole to pick up on my uneasiness, and after the first few days, whenever she'd hear me coming, if she was exposed, she'd cover herself up, or turn over on her stomach. I appreciated that."

Later, she might start to warm up in preparation for a run. Often, two of her girlfriends, Cora Fischman and Cici Shahian, would come by and get ready with her, and all three would take off for the San Vicente route.

After a run, she would spend the rest of the morning and part of the afternoon lying out in the sun, usually until a little before three when it was time to pick up the kids at school.

Both Sydney and Justin attended private institutions. Justin was a preschooler at the Sunshine School, while Sydney, who was in the second grade, went to nearby Carlthorpe. Often, on the way home, Nicole would run errands. After the kids changed their clothes and got cleaned up, either Nicole or Maria would start dinner.

Nicole rarely watched television. On those nights she didn't go out, she'd put the kids to bed by 8:30 and get into her own big, black wrought-iron bed under a thick downy comforter and read a book. There was always one nearby, opened to the page she was on. If she was really into it, she'd carry a copy around with her during the day, pick it up, read a few pages, put it down, and be able fall right back into it the next chance she got.

"She told me she particularly loved books about the inner self," Kato recounted, "such as *Men Are from Mars, Women Are from Venus*. She seemed quite affected by that one. She also liked *Iron John* a lot. She told me that these books were infinitely more helpful to her than any of those group-therapy sessions she'd attended. She also began writing poetry, and seemed quite enthusiastic about trying to put her private thoughts down on paper."

Her parents often came up from Dana Point to visit. Judi, her mother, was there more than her father, who worked (for one of O.J.'s companies) during the day. Her sisters Denise and Dominique and Denise's child Sean, would also visit (Tanya, the youngest, almost never did). Whenever any of them saw Kato, they were always very cordial, as he was to them.

There seemed to be an especially strong bond between Judi and Nicole. Some days they'd go out and spend the afternoon shopping, getting their nails done, or just passing the time having a leisurely lunch. Or, they'd just sit by the pool and talk for hours. Kato often heard Nicole tell her mother how hard a time she was having trying to decide whether or not to reconcile with O.J.

This surprised him, since he thought their relationship was completely over. Not only were she and O.J. divorced, but to Kato, Nicole seemed much more upset over her failed relationship with Grant than she did about her divorce from O.J. One time Kato heard her tell her mother that she and O.J. were considering marriage counseling, to see if they could work things out and get back together. According to Kato, Judi couldn't understand what the problem was. "Nicole," she said, "it's so simple. I just want to see you happy. If getting back together with O.J. will make you happy, then fine, do it. If it won't, then you should move on."

Nicole, however, seemed unable to make any kind of firm decision and remained ambivalent about O.J. The longer Kato lived at Gretna Green, the more he began to pick up on the complexity of Nicole's ongoing relationship with O.J. One day she would wake up all bright and happy and tell Kato she was falling in love again with O.J., only to change her mood and mind completely the next, saying she never wanted to see her ex-husband again.

Kato began to feel that maybe one of the problems was a

191

conflict of loyalties. It seemed obvious to him that her family wasn't that anxious for Nicole to completely sever her ties from O.J. He had, after all, according to Kato, provided Lou Brown, Nicole's father, with a secure job at a Hertz franchise, and Rolf, husband of Nicole's housekeeper, Maria, with another at one at his Pioneer Chicken outlets. In addition, O.J. had supposedly paid Tanya's college tuition. It is questionable how much encouragement Nicole's family provided during her attempt to break out of O.J.'s iron grip. "As I look back now," Kato said, "I wonder how much real emotional support Nicole actually got from her family, especially after spousal abuse became an issue in their marriage. It's frightening and sad to me to think Nicole may have been crying out for a type of support no one in her world recognized as a plea for help, or was willing to give to her, until it was too late."

Although Maria usually prepared dinner during the week, Nicole loved to putter around in the kitchen. So did the kids. Sydney, especially, relished getting her hands into the raw ingredients of some complex recipe and goo herself all up. If she tried to pour a bowl of ingredients into a large pot, half of it would usually wind up on the floor, or on the walls. By the end of the evening, the kitchen would be a total mess, with half-cooked food and dirty pots and pans everywhere. They'd be like three kids, one big and two little, playing in a gigantic mudpuddle.

This was in marked contrast to how Kato saw them behave whenever O.J. came over. The kids always had to be on their best behavior. O.J. didn't like it when they became too rambunctious. With Nicole, they could get away with anything. With O.J., they got away with nothing.

On evenings Nicole wanted to go out, if he were going to be

home, Kato would often volunteer to watch Justin and Sydney. She pretty much trusted him about everything and was quite casual about his presence in the house. She thought nothing of leaving piles of cash around, or letting Kato have the security code. And of course, she had no problem trusting the safety of the kids to him.

So much so that for the first two months, she didn't charge any rent. The deal between them was quite informal, nothing in writing. If Kato did enough baby-sitting and handiwork around the house, Nicole considered it sufficient compensation.

At first, the arrangement seemed perfect, especially to Kato. Here he was, living rent-free, with Nicole throwing a lot of expensive parties, introducing him to a whole new world. As far as he could tell, she was happy, well-off, out for a good time.

As it turned out, she was none of those things. By the third month, the arrangement had broken down, primarily because Nicole, who loved to spend money, simply began to run out of it, and needed to earn income from the guest house to help cover her expenses. Moreover, Kato didn't like feeling obligated to staying home at night, especially on the weekends. After some friendly negotiating, it was agreed that Kato would pay five hundred dollars a month as a base rent, with any baby-sitting time to be deducted from that figure.

There's no question that Kato still had a great deal. However, everything being relative, because he wasn't earning very much money, it was difficult to meet his commitment.

When Kato was late with his first month's rent, Nicole became quite annoyed. It didn't help matters any that it was a particularly stressing time for her in terms of trying to deal with O.J. She decided to approach the subject indirectly, telling Kato that one of the things that had really made her angry was O.J.'s reneging on his promise to pay the children's school tuition, insisting it was included in the $24,000 a month he was already paying for child support (later reduced to $17,000 and then $10,000 a month). When it came to the kids, she told Kato, "he wasn't a great father. He was never really around."

It was simply too difficult for Nicole to confront Kato one-on-one. Instead, she left a handwritten note for him in which she spelled out the facts of her financial life.

She began by expressing sympathy for Kato's economic bind, but reiterated that she, too, was having difficulties making ends meet. She reminded him that he had already lived at the house for two months essentially rent-free, and that in two weeks he was going to owe *another* month's rent.

She broke down her own expenses for him: $4,800 rent for the house; $1,230 for Justin's school; $3,300 for Sydney's; $800 a month for Maria. Water and power came to $450, gas $250. Then there was food, phone, car insurance, health insurance, car payments, property taxes, uniforms, hot lunch, programs for school, gasoline, clothing for herself and the kids, in addition to "the regular, everyday things." She closed by saying she felt bad, but "I can't feel sorry for you, cuz I already feel sorry for me."

She signed the letter "Nick," a smiley face underneath.

She left it on Kato's bed. When he read it, he was a bit confused. He thought they had a great, open relationship, and could talk to each other about anything. He made it his business to get the money he owed her the next day. When he handed it to her, he could tell she was a bit embarrassed by the whole episode. Sensing her discomfort, Kato said, "Nicole, please don't feel afraid to tell me anything. If I screw up, you can tell me, we're friends. I'm really sorry about what happened."

"Kato," she said with a regretful whine in her voice, "I feel so sorry for writing that letter. . . . "

It turned out not to affect the friendship adversely. Once Kato paid off his debt, it was never mentioned again. Nor did he ever miss another rent deadline.

In May 1993, Nicole decided to throw a party for her birthday and bring her friends together with Kato's so everyone could meet the other side of their respective worlds.

Things didn't work out exactly as planned. Kato's friends may have been as much into money and status as Nicole's, but they went about their quests in an entirely different fashion. No fancy clothes, or expensive jewelry, no elaborate hairdos. Kato's was a crowd of mostly actors and actresses who liked to work hard (when they got work) and play hard. Nicole's was a mostly divorced, upper-middle, upper-upper crowd of men in their hard fifties and women rapidly approaching their dreaded forties.

Kato rarely socialized with Nicole's inner circle of girl-friends, headed by Faye Resnick and Cici Shahian. A third, Cora Fischman, was the only one besides Nicole he felt could relate to. The two had met while Cora was still married to her husband, Ron, and were O.J. and Nicole's neighbors on Rockingham. The women remained friends after their respective marriages fell apart. The strongest bond between them was motherhood. Cora's child, Leslie, attended the same school as Sydney, and the two had become best friends. They both danced together in the June 12 recital.

The other two, Kato felt, saw men as objects of security rather than human beings worthy of love. All, including Nicole, had been married and divorced at least once. "Soap-opera characters in a soap-opera town," Kato called them.

Cici was perhaps the most desperate of the four. Faye and Cora didn't get along with each other, and made no secret of their feelings, even in front of a crowd. In fact, the entire pretentious circle was in reality a series of minicircles, with no one liking everyone else in the group. Faye struck Kato as the least sincere, never satisfied with anyone or anything, a friend of Nicole's only because she was married to "somebody famous," and constantly on the lookout for a "better" man than the one she happened to be with. In addition, it seemed they were all trying to date younger men, and one-upping each other in the process. They had two categories: the men they wanted to have sex with and the men they wanted to marry. Long-term worth was measured by a bank account, short-term worth by . . . other yardsticks.

Finally, when these women did get into "relationships," it seemed to Kato they always had to be the one in charge. He would never forget seeing one of the most famous athletes in the world, renowned for his physical strength and endurance, being bossed around by one of the weakest women he'd ever met. It was a scene he didn't understand, or belong to.

One evening, Nicole and Faye were out barhopping, feeling no pain. Nicole was driving her Ferrari, for which, after the divorce, she'd gotten new plates, L84AD8. After leaving one club, they got into the car and Nicole accidentally rammed into the one in front of her, which then caught on fire. During the confusion, as Nicole's story went, Faye insisted they switch seats so Nicole, who'd already had her share of run-ins with the LAPD, wouldn't get into more trouble for driving while under the influence.

To Nicole, this was a supreme gesture of friendship. When she told Kato about it, his first reaction was how foolish and wrongheaded the whole thing sounded. Maybe, he thought to himself (but didn't express to Nicole), it would have been better for her to have been arrested. It might have forced her to deal with one of the problems she had trouble admitting existed. Nicole had a tendency to drink a little too much.

Thursday nights, "girls' night out," Nicole and the others frequented a regular circuit of clubs on Sunset Boulevard in Beverly Hills. After coming home one night a little tipsy, Nicole told Kato how Faye had met Don Henley at Bar One and was sure he was crazy about her. Nicole said she shook her head, laughed, and told Faye to get real. Faye continued, unfazed, openly fantasizing about the wonderful relationship she was sure she and Henley were going to have.

If, on one of her nights on the town, Nicole happened to meet someone she liked, as soon as she got home she would tell Kato all the breathless details. Still, as happy as he'd be for her, Kato never believed Nicole could find a new life's companion in the nightclubs of Los Angeles. She was, after all, approaching her midthirties, and the L.A. bar scene was filled with young actresses and model types in their twenties. Kato felt Nicole was really being dragged along by the others, all of whom seemed to be endlessly searching for the perfect one-night stand. "You know, Nicole," he would tell her, "I honestly don't think you're going to meet the man of your dreams at any of those places." He'd remember later how she would turn away when he said such things, and stare off into space.

Occasionally, Nicole would meet someone at the most unexpected places. Church, for example. One day she came home all excited and told Kato, "I met this new guy, he's so good-looking and we got along so well. I'm going to go back next week, and I hope he's there." Kato smiled, shook his head, and thought to himself, as did everyone else, that Nicole was forever in search of perfect love.

Every so often, Kato would bring a friend over to meet Nicole. "I never wanted to interfere with her desire to reconcile with O.J., but I believed that Nicole was fully capable of making her own decisions and acting like the adult she was."

Not very often, but occasionally, at Nicole's insistence, Kato would go out for dinner with her and one of her girlfriends, and bring along one of his buddies to even the numbers.

One time he went to dinner at Mezzaluna with Nicole and Cici and invited a friend of his to join them. While eating Kato noticed three young girls having drinks at a nearby table. Nicole, meanwhile, was drinking tequila, and after a while it began to show.

"Suddenly, out of nowhere, she said she knew one of the girls at that other table and couldn't stand her. Moreover, she was convinced they were talking about her. She also said something bitchy about how young they were, which I figured was maybe what was really bothering her.

"Nicole kept on doing shots, and I began to worry that something was going to happen. I didn't enjoy her when she got like that, and usually didn't hang around to see very much of it. When I realized she was not going to let it go, I decided to split. In spite of all the garbage that has been written elsewhere, that was about the extent of my nighttime socializing with Nicole."

As the year passed, Kato became an increasingly important figure in Nicole's life. She'd often knock on his guest-house bedroom door when she'd come in from a night out, no matter how late the hour, to find out if he was asleep. If he wasn't, or she could wake him, she'd insist he come over to her place to talk. Kato never refused her, no matter how tired he was. He'd splash some cold water on his face, throw some clothes on, and join her.

Other times, she'd be lying in bed, unable to sleep, and

would go have a cigarette on the balcony. If she saw the light on in the guest house, she'd figure Kato was awake and call out his name. If he popped his head out, she'd ask him what he was up to. From the tone in her voice, he could usually tell if she wanted him to come over.

"She'd always begin by apologizing in case she was interrupting me," he recalled. "Then she'd ask me what I was up to, and we'd often end up talking until dawn. We'd talk about everything that was going on in both our lives. It was during these sessions that Nicole confided all her hopes, fears, and desires."

Among them was her desire to one day run a coffee shop. It seemed an entirely plausible idea to her, especially since O.J. had a handful of successful chicken and ham outlets around Los Angeles and, until the Rodney King riots destroyed many of them, had done quite well. The coffee shop was a way for her to prove she could make it on her own, without O.J., no matter how modest the enterprise might be.

Originally, she planned to open a Starbucks in partnership with Faye Resnick. At the time the franchised coffee bars were springing up all over L.A., and Nicole often hung out at the one in Brentwood.

Kato thought it was a terrific idea and told her so. She became excited about it, until it came time to actually do something to make the dream real. The major problem was financing. According to what Nicole told Kato, Faye couldn't come up with her half of the start-up money.

It wouldn't have been so bad, except that Nicole didn't have hers either. At first she thought about asking O.J. for a loan, but decided against it, she told Kato, because she knew what his answer would be. He was always against her actually *doing* anything, especially having a real job. He didn't mind if she dabbled in interior decoration, and even lined up a few of his friends to hire her to redo their homes. However, he never wanted anyone to think she *had* to work, because that might look as if he wasn't able to take good enough care of her.

Everything had to be O.J.'s way, or no way, she told Kato. She called her ex-husband "the king of manipulation. You have to see him work." She said so many negative things about him that when she'd then start talking about reconciling, Kato would wonder where it was coming from.

When the Starbucks idea fell through, Nicole talked about opening a small, nonfranchised coffee shop on her own. She went so far as to actually pick out a location and had hoped that Keith Zlomsowitch might run it for her. To raise start-up money, she'd decided to sell the San Francisco town house O.J. had acquired when he played for the 49ers and had given to her as part of their divorce settlement. He no longer had any use for it, and felt it would be a solid long-term investment for Nicole and the kids. And it didn't cost him anything to give it up.

For one reason or another, the coffee shop never happened, and after a while she stopped talking about it. As Kato was to discover, Nicole was someone who loved to dream about doing things, but somehow rarely got around to realizing those dreams. And sometimes that wasn't such a bad thing.

"One night," Kato told me, "she couldn't sleep and called me over for one of our talks. At one point she looked at me and said, 'Kato, I want to ask you a question. What do you think about two girls being together?'

"I laughed and said it wasn't my thing.

"'There's this one woman,' she went on, 'I have a hard time telling you this, but I'm very attracted to her physically and I can't figure out why. Whenever I see her around, I get this funny feeling, and I know she has the same feeling for me.' She went on to tell me that she loved great bodies, male or female, preferred men, but couldn't deny this feeling she had for this one woman."

Not all her confessions were quite fantasies or isolated.

"Nicole loved sex. . . . One night she told me a story about what happened when she first started dating O.J. He was still married to his wife, Marguerite. One horrible day their daughter accidentally drowned in the family swimming pool. [Nicole] couldn't understand why O.J. wasn't more upset by it. One of the most incredible things to her was the fact that, although she didn't know what had happened until later, O.J. made love to her that same night. She said that if anything ever happened to one of her children, she wouldn't be able to go on living. She'd have to kill herself.

"She often talked to me about how different her life was when she was married to O.J., how she had never cheated on him, not even once, had never thought about it, never dared to. She said when they first got married she was totally in love with him, and felt completely committed. She told me she had met him when she was only seventeen years old, and now, as she looked back at the age of thirty-four, realized how much she had missed, especially the kind of things single women do in their late teens and twenties. She'd never really dated anyone but O.J. She didn't go to college. She never had a job. She had no career. She didn't travel with a group of girlfriends to see the world. She went from being a teenager to O.J.'s woman, first as his girlfriend, then as his live-in lover, and finally his wife."

After they divorced, she said, she felt as if she had a lot of lost time to make up for. She told Kato how only recently she had come to feel she was finally ready to accept the fact that she could be sexually attracted to other men besides O.J. Especially young ones.

Kato says she was after him to set her up with good-looking guys in their early twenties. She had certain looks she liked, which she described as "soap-opera-ish," young, cute,

201

fresh-looking boys, or the dark, Italian-stud types. There was one in particular on daytime TV she had her eye on, a handsome young fellow by the name of Antonio Sabato, Jr. "Do you know him?" she asked Kato. He said he didn't and she said, on more than one occasion, "I'd sure like to meet him."

There were times when the conversation was less fanciful and more filled with fear. On many nights Nicole told Kato that O.J. had people spying on her, that her life was in danger.

"Come on, Nicole, you can't be serious," Kato would reply.

She'd insist, however, that she wasn't making it up, that it was all true. She even suspected that O.J. was spying on her while she had sex with other men, that he was having her sessions videotaped. "He told me he videotaped me making love in my bedroom with someone one time," she told Kato. She used to warn him that his phone was tapped, that he was probably being videotaped as well, that he taking a chance, that his own life was in danger just by virtue of having moved into the guest house. One night, she turned to him matter-of-factly and stated in a flat voice that she was "sure O.J. is going to kill me one day." She told Kato that O.J. had guns "everywhere in his house. You don't know him, Kato."

He thought she was exaggerating and being overly dramatic, to impress him with how obsessed O.J. still was with her. Kato tried to laugh it off, but as she continued he began to realize she wasn't kidding, that she wasn't playing games. If no one else was going to, it became clear to Kato that Nicole was taking herself and the precarious state of her relations with O.J. very seriously. "If he even saw us driving around together," which they occasionally did, in the Ferrari O.J. had bought Nicole, "he'd really be pissed. . . . I can't believe the power he has over people," she told Kato. "Because he's a celebrity, because he's O.J. Simpson. No one's going to touch him. *O.J. Simpson can get away with murder!"*

Her mood would often take wide swings. Later on, O.J. would describe Nicole to Kato as the type of person who could be so happy one day, go out and drink, have a blast, and the next day undergo a total emotional reversal. Kato had to agree with that. It was obvious to him that she seemed to live only for the next party, and the day after would usually be a bit moody and depressed, until preparations for a new one began.

Kato saw this reflected in the way she related to O.J.'s attempts at reconciliation. Sometimes she'd become annoyed at him for calling too often. He'd phone every day when he was out of town, to tell her he loved her and wanted to know what she was doing. She'd tell him not to call so often, that her routine was the same every day. Then, when he'd stop calling, she'd wonder why. It was as if no matter what he did, it wasn't going to be right.

If she and O.J. were planning a trip, she'd get all excited about it, spend a whole day packing, arrive in some new, exotic place, have a ball, and then when they'd return, fall into a funk until the next significant event in her life approached.

She told Kato about how life with O.J. wasn't as glamorous as he might think. She said he had a violent temper and often took out his frustrations on her. She told him O.J. was one of the most physically powerful men she'd ever met. "You don't know how strong he is," she told Kato, who had no trouble believing that the first time he shook The Juice's hand.

"You really have to see him in action to understand what I'm talking about," she said. She told Kato about one time when she was sitting at a bar and a guy tried to pick her up. Nicole said he was pretty big and mean looking but that O.J. came over, literally raised him off the floor by his lapels, and hurled him across the room.

She told him about the many (unreported) times he'd beaten her up and how, when she was pregnant with Sydney, he'd tell her she was too fat. One time he'd picked up a woman, snuck her into the Rockingham estate, brought her into one of the guest houses, and made love to her. Nicole caught him in the act, and his reaction was, hey, no big deal. She said he was constantly trying to prove how much of a man he was. To that end, he often made love to her several times a day. "Our relationship was based purely on sex," she'd say, and admitted that in the beginning it had been one of their strongest bonds. She admitted she was as much a sex maniac as he was.

In May 1993, Nicole agreed to go with O.J. to Cabo San Lucas, in yet another of their seemingly endless attempts at reconciliation. When they returned, Nicole told Kato how awful the first two days had been. "It began as one of the worst trips of my life," she said. The reason, she explained, was that O.J. had set out to prove that he was still able to satisfy her sexually. He insisted upon making love to her five times a day, she said, violently, all the while screaming, *"I'll do you like no one else can do you!"*

She told Kato she begged him to ease up. "O.J., please, give me a break." She said it wasn't until the third day that he just physically wore himself out.

Kato wondered what it would be like when he and O.J. finally met. That time came one morning in February. O.J. had a habit of showing up unannounced at Gretna Green, which, Kato learned later, had caused Nicole some embarrassment.

When she first moved in, a couple of her neighbors called the police to report a "black" prowler around her house. They didn't know at the time that she had been married to O.J. and, although divorced, was on "friendly" terms, and that O.J. had liberal visitation rights to the children. Nicole had no use for that kind of thinking. She was sure the neighbors' reaction was rooted in racial prejudice, that if they had seen a white man they wouldn't have thought twice about it. She preferred her own circle of friends, and to that end never became very close to her neighbors.

The Brentwood problem was not limited to neighbors. There was a fire station not very far from the house. Several of the firemen got to know Nicole and eventually one asked who "this black guy" was that kept coming to visit. When she explained it was O.J. Simpson and that he was her ex-husband, they stopped coming by.

Kato's first meeting with O.J. was, in fact, not the warmest of occasions. Kato was in the yard playing softball with Justin, trying to teach him how to throw, when out of the corner of his eye he saw O.J. walking toward the back of the house. He remembered noticing that O.J. kept his head down, as if he didn't want to see anyone, or anyone to see him. When he passed by Kato, he grunted something that sounded vaguely like hello.

"Hey, I'm Kato."

O.J. looked up. "Oh yeah, how you doin', Kato?"

"Dad!" Justin screamed.

"Go say hello to your father," Kato said. Justin ran up to O.J. and they both went to the front of the house to wait for Nicole, who'd stepped out for a few minutes.

There was a definite chill. It hadn't been the friendliest of meetings. Kato got the message that O.J. didn't want any company as he waited for Nicole to return.

"A fellow by the name of T. K. Carter used to come by and visit a lot," Kato recalled. "He's a well-known comedian, and shortly after I met him I began writing jokes with him. He used to take me aside and ask me if anything was going on between Nicole and me. I'd tell him absolutely not. He told me he thought she was pretty hot, but knew O.J. and wouldn't be crazy enough to ever try anything. 'The Juice would cream me.' After my first encounter, I knew exactly what he meant." Kato missed what might have very well been a gang-style message of warning sent to him by an always wary and possessive O.J.

Kato knew that even before that first day, O.J. had become aware of the fact that "some guy" was living in the guest house, and it bothered him. Cathy Randa, O.J.'s personal assistant, had told Kato as much one day when she'd come over to discuss something with Nicole about an upcoming visit with the kids.

Cathy and Kato hit it off, became friendly, and one time when she called the house, he happened to answer the phone. They chatted for a while, and then she told Kato that O.J. had asked about him. He'd wanted to know about "this Kato guy." She said he had been reassured by everyone he'd asked, including her, that he was okay. "After I met him," Kato remembered, "I spoke to Cathy again and she said he told her he hadn't wanted to like me, but realized I was no threat. We got to know each other a little and he told her, 'You're right, Kato's a good guy.'"

After the football season ended and O.J.'s announcing chores lightened up, he came by to visit the kids quite often. The more he saw of Kato, the friendlier the two became. He never came out and directly asked, but he seemed confident that nothing was going on between his ex-wife and her houseguest. As a result, his demeanor toward Kato changed. He began to smile a lot more, joke around a little, and show the side of his personality that, in Kato's words, "simply dazzled."

———

O.J. worked steadily, if not impressively, in a number of films. What had begun as an attempt at "serious" acting in features like *Towering Inferno* quickly dissipated into mindless comedies. O.J. wound up playing roles that spoofed his own physical image. Worse, his performances never impressed Nicole. She was always chiding him about not making "real" movies. She declined to accompany him to their star-studded premieres.

One day O.J. came by and invited Kato to watch the filming of a scene from *Naked Gun 33 1/3*. Kato eagerly accepted the offer. His first impression on the set was of how many people hovered around O.J., seeming to hang on his every word.

Filming was at the Shrine Auditorium, directly across the boulevard from O.J.'s alma mater, USC. The scene was supposedly the Academy Awards. In it, Leslie Nielsen is holding an envelope with a bomb concealed in it. O.J. plays one of the cops who shows up to try to prevent it from going off.

Between takes, O.J. introduced Kato to Nielsen and Olympia Dukakis, and even let him sit in his director's chair, which Kato got a real kick out of.

Nielsen is a practical joker. He had this battery device in his coat that made a sound like farting. All the while between setups, he'd start talking to someone, and the sounds of farts would come from the machine. Kato found this hysterical, although everyone else seemed to react as if they'd long ago grown tired of the gag.

Kato spent a lot of time that day hanging out with O.J. in his trailer, talking and having a great time. At one point during the afternoon, O.J. told him he had this girl coming by, a real knockout, and that Kato would go nuts over her. Sure enough, a gorgeous young woman did knock on the door, and Kato could tell it was his cue to leave.

Later on, O.J., in a casual, almost joking manner, reminded Kato that he was still living at Nicole's and of course there were certain things he just couldn't tell her. Kato reassured him that he had nothing to worry about, that he would never do anything like that. Besides, he said, why would it matter? After all, they were no longer married.

"It matters," O.J. said.

Another time during the filming, O.J. invited Kato to the Paramount studios on Melrose Avenue in Hollywood. One of O.J.'s golfing buddies happened to come by. He and Kato talked for a while, and he told Kato how great it was to hang with O.J., just hoping to pick up the throwaways.

The end of the football season affected Nicole in more ways than one. Kato noticed that in March, Marcus Allen began coming over to the house to visit her quite often. O.J. had been Marcus's mentor, big brother, and best friend. According to Nicole, he had practically brought Marcus up, and gotten him into and guided him through USC and pro football. Marcus worshiped O.J. and everything about him—including, as Kato soon discovered—Nicole. It probably didn't help matters any that O.J. had bragged to Marcus about what a great sexual partner she was.

She said she and Marcus had quite a lot in common, especially a certain type of spirituality, which she said she really loved about him. When she suspected, however, that he might have a physical thing for her, she told Kato that while she liked Marcus, they could never become emotionally involved, and for a number of reasons, not the least being their respective relationships with O.J.

Nicole and Marcus often went out during the day to have some innocent fun. One time he came by, asked Nicole if she felt like doing something, and she suggested they all go shoot some pool down at the Gotham Hall in the Santa Monica Third Street Promenade.

Kato was home at the time and Nicole invited him and a friend of his, Kelly, who happened to have dropped by, to come along.

They all went to the pool hall and were shooting racks, relaxing, and knocking back a few tequilas. Marcus, who doesn't drink, kept pouring his shots into Nicole's glass when she wasn't looking. It didn't take very long for her to develop a bit of a buzz.

She began hanging on to Marcus, then on to Kato, and after a while it was hard to tell who was with whom. At one point, Nicole suggested they all go back to the house. Once there, she went into the kitchen to prepare some refreshments, and asked Kato to give her a hand.

In the kitchen, she turned and said to Kato, "I have to tell you something and I don't know how to say it."

He couldn't imagine what was on her mind. Had his rent check bounced? Then he flashed on the possibility that she was going to confess how she'd fallen in love with Marcus and wanted some advice.

"I don't know how to tell you this," she repeated, "but I'm falling in love with you."

Kato felt the blood drain from his face. He couldn't believe what he was hearing. "No, you're not," he said.

"Yes, I am," she insisted. "I've had dreams about you." He remembered now how sometimes in the mornings he'd met Nicole in her kitchen for coffee and she'd say, "Whoa, you don't want to be around me today. . . . I had a dream about you, and you don't want to know what it was."

"Come on," he'd say, thinking she was teasing him. "Were we . . . doing things? Was I good?"

He remembered how she'd laugh, and that would be it. Now, though, she wasn't laughing.

"No, uh, hey, listen, Nicole, I love you, too. As a friend. But we could never be . . . romantically involved. I couldn't do it." He meant it. He insisted he wasn't sexually attracted to her, and was canny enough to know it could never work any other way between them than the way it was now.

"But, Kato," she went on, "it's perfect. The kids love you. . . ."

"Nicole," he said, groping for excuses, "I'm not a wealthy guy. I live in the guest house, remember? I'm the guy who was late with his rent!"

"You're going to be very famous one day soon, Kato," she replied. "I can feel it."

"Yeah, and I'll be able to afford to move into a larger guest house!"

He was trying to keep things light by cracking jokes, but he was thrown. He began to think about how protective Nicole had always seemed. It then occurred to him that he might actually have to move out because of this.

Nicole sensed his unease. "I know you're uncomfortable about what I've said," she told him, "but I had to say it." With that, she smiled and went back into the living room.

Kato pulled himself together as best he could and joined them. Nicole put some music on and they all started to dance. At the first opportunity Kato grabbed Kelly by the hand and took her back to the guest house.

It has been reported elsewhere that Marcus and Nicole had a "blazing sexual relationship," which was probably true. Certainly they dallied, but kept it to a minimum. Without question, Nicole knew what buttons to push when it came to doing sexual battle with O.J. In that sense, he was a "perfect" lover for Nicole.

She told Kato of at least one occasion when Marcus had come on to her, and she let him know the strict parameters of friendship she wanted to keep between them. Although she let him masturbate on her breasts, she told Kato, there could never be anything serious between them because of O.J.

Eventually, Marcus got the message, or at least what part of it he wanted to hear. Thereafter, whenever he visited Nicole, he'd park his car several blocks away so that if O.J. happened to drive by, he wouldn't know Allen was there. All of this bothered Nicole, and she spent several nights discussing it with Kato at great length.

Somehow, O.J. managed to get wind of her "friendship" with Marcus, and it caused a huge fight between O.J. and Nicole. That June, Marcus got married to a beautiful blonde named Katherine. O.J. insisted that the wedding be held at the Rockingham estate. Nicole was noticeably absent from both the ceremony and the reception.

Kato sensed the morning after Nicole's "confession of love" was going to be a difficult one. In fact, the next several mornings were filled with awkwardness. She would see him and act with an extreme politeness they both knew was defensive and artificial. Finally, three or four days later, she asked if they could talk. Kato said sure, and they went to her living room.

They sat down on the sofa and Nicole told him she was sorry about what she'd said and hoped it hadn't damaged their friendship. "I can get over it," she assured Kato.

He was so relieved that he put an arm around her shoulder and said, "Nicole, I hope you know I would do anything for you."

She told him she was beginning to think that sometimes maybe she drank a little too much and, when she did, lost a bit of self-control. That, she was certain, was what the other day had really been all about. She knew it was a sign of

211

weakness on her part, and one of the ways people used to take advantage of her.

She was right about that. Kato had seen it happen many times. Besides Marcus Allen, there was the Faye Resnick situation. It seemed to Kato that Faye was forever using Nicole for one thing or another, and afterward, Nicole would complain to him that she knew what Faye was up to, but hadn't known what to do about it.

For instance, Faye was forever selling things out of her apartment—purses, ties, jewelry. One part of her condo was set up like a boutique in a department store. She was always asking Nicole to buy things from her and to bring her rich friends along to see what was available.

And, Nicole was certain, Faye had eyes for Kato. One time Nicole told him this, adding that she considered him a really good friend and hoped he wouldn't do anything with Faye. Kato assured her he had no interest in the woman. "Fine," Nicole said. "As long as you don't date Cici either!" That brought a smile to both their faces, and laid to rest any lingering tension from the afternoon of Nicole's "confession."

O.J. liked to throw an annual summer party every June, and in 1993, invited Kato to attend. It was the first time he met O.J.'s circle of friends, including Robert Kardashian, Mark Slotkin, and Ron Fischman.

In O.J.'s living room, everyone participated in parlor games that had an adult edge to them. In one, a form of *Truth or Dare,* the men would sit on one side, the women on the other, and they'd make up questions like "Where did you have your first sexual experience?" The questions would then be put into a big hat, everyone would reach for one, and have to answer what he or she pulled out.

O.J., Kato recalled, seemed extremely happy that day. He told Kato it reminded him of the way thing used to be, Nicole by his side, everyone having fun. It was, in fact, one of the few times Kato saw the positive chemistry that must have brought the two together in their earlier, happier days.

Nicole, too, seemed to be having a wonderful time. At one point Kato saw them arm in arm, and thought, for the first time, hey, maybe they can make it together after all.

Early in October, O.J. took Nicole to the opening of the Harley-Davidson Café in New York City. Faye Resnick was there, with her boyfriend at the time, Christian Reichardt, all on O.J.'s nickel. Often, when they'd travel together, O.J. and Nicole would invite a couple of friends along to make it seem even more like a party.

When they returned to Los Angeles from the opening, Nicole showed Kato a series of Polaroids taken at the party. She pointed out a good-looking young fellow she'd been attracted to, and who, she claimed, was attracted to her. Kato was surprised and said, "You were with O.J. and flirting with someone else?"

"Yes," she said animatedly. "He was this Italian-looking model type and I was like—oh, Kato, I wanted him!" She told Kato he'd slipped her a note that she had to be very careful to keep hidden from O.J.

It always made Kato uneasy to hear about the "chances" Nicole took, and how, somehow, Faye Resnick was always around when these things happened. O.J. believed Resnick was the reason Nicole was developing interests in so many other men, that Faye encouraged her to go out and play the field. On the other hand, Kato wondered, why would O.J. have allowed someone he so disapproved of to come along in the first place?

And, of course, the same stories, with minor variations, would come from the other side of the white picket fence. A week after the trip, O.J. told Kato about the same opening-night party. "Kato, man, I'm telling you, there were some girls at this thing . . . one of them was just all over me. . . . "

Early in the evening of October 25, 1993, Kato was coming home from working out at his health club when, as he drove down Gretna Green, he happened to notice O.J.'s Bronco parked at a weird angle, blocking the driveway. Its flashers were still on. He figured O.J. must have hurriedly dropped by to pick something up.

As Kato pulled up and walked toward the guest house, he suddenly heard loud screaming coming from the backyard. He looked toward the house and saw the French doors to the den wide open. Just then, O.J., in shirt, shorts, and sandals, turned and saw Kato walk by, looked at him for a second, turned and continued to yell, pacing back and forth in the kitchen, where Nicole, in jeans and tank top, was on the phone, frantically trying to get the police to send help.

"What are you doing to me . . . What are you doing . . . you make me take all my pictures of Paula down and you still got some guy in the den. . . . " O.J. also railed about stories in *The National Enquirer. "You can't believe all those goddamn papers, those tabloids always have stories about me. . . . "*

At first Kato decided to stay out of it and went into the guest house. Before he closed the door, however, he took another look to make sure Nicole was all right, and realized that O.J. was still in a rage. O.J.'s yelling became louder as he moved closer to her. Kato decided he had to do something after all.

He came back out and started walking toward the kitchen. He wanted O.J. to notice him, hoping to shift his focus away from Nicole. Sure enough, as soon as O.J. saw Kato coming, he turned and continued his harangue, shouting as if he were trying somehow to convince Kato that he, O.J., was really the wronged party in all of this.

"How can she blow some guy while my children are upstairs . . . ? What kind of woman is this . . . ? What's going on . . . ?"

"What are you talking about, O.J.? Are you okay, man?"

"They print these articles about me and some woman in the Enquirer, *it's a lie. . . . Those tabloids are always saying things about me that are lies . . . lies. . . . How can you believe them?"*

Kato had no idea what he was talking about. He noticed that O.J. was standing just to the right of a door which led directly to a guest bedroom, and that it was closed. Kato thought to himself, My God, there must be a guy in that room, O.J.'s caught Nicole with another man!

Just then, as if he was able to read Kato's mind, O.J. turned and reached for the door. It was locked and Kato flashed on how if there someone was in there, it wasn't going to be pretty.

By now, O.J.'s face was sweaty, his eyes bulging with fury, a vein was popping in his temple. Kato then noticed for the first time that the French doors had been smashed, and realized O.J. had busted his way into Nicole's house.

During all of this, Nicole remained on the phone, desperately trying to get the 911 operator to send help. *"Kato,"* O.J. finally cried, as if his anger was finally beginning to subside.

The police arrived a short time later. The first thing they wanted to know was whether anybody was hurt. The second was, who Kato was. "What's your story?" one of them said to him in a not totally friendly manner.

"It's just Kato," O.J. said. "He lives in the guest house. He's cool." The police then decided the guest house was as good a place as any to use for neutral territory. Two of them took O.J. and Kato there while two others went to try to calm Nicole down.

In the guest house, the police seemed friendly to O.J. "What's going on?" one of them asked, in a quiet, casual tone.

O.J. shook his head slowly and said, "This woman thing . . . "

"Yeah," the officer said. "I'm married, too. I know what you mean." They kept O.J. talking, and eventually Kato excused himself. He wanted to see how Nicole was faring.

He found her still in the kitchen, crying as she told the two policemen that she didn't want to see O.J. anymore. She didn't calm down until they assured her that he would leave the premises without coming back inside the house.

The police stayed with Nicole for quite a while, during which time she showed them the damage O.J. had done to the French doors. One of the officers asked Kato if he could fix them. He said he thought so, found a hammer and nails, and began to bang them back onto their wooden frame. (Weeks later Nicole would tell Kato that among the many things that remained unresolved between O.J. and her was that he had promised to pay for the replacement of those French doors but never had).

After the police left, Kato continued to try to make repairs, while Nicole, still upset, began talking. She said she couldn't believe the kids had slept through the whole noisy altercation. When she was still married to O.J., she told Kato, they used to fight all the time in front of the children, who would become frightened and start to cry. It got to a point where Sydney, in Nicole's words, "was so used to the fighting, it became a normal part of her life, which is why she had to have a security blanket and continually sucked on her fingers." Nicole said that during the really bad fights, Sydney would take her blanket, lie down, and suck on her fingers until she fell asleep.

Nicole went on to say that Sydney also developed a habit of sleepwalking. Often, she would get up early in the evening, looking completely asleep, go to the refrigerator, reach for some ice cream, put it down on the table, and go back to bed. It is an odd story, but one that throws light on the unexplained presence of the cup of ice cream that would later cause the prosecution to go into a frenzy of theorizing.

Nicole also told Kato that what he'd seen that evening wasn't the first example of O.J.'s violent anger and that she was tired of it all. One night, she said, they'd had a huge fight in front of her sister Denise, which quickly became physical. At one point, O.J. actually picked up Nicole and threw her out of the house. She'd landed on her "butt and elbows" and was sore for days.

The thing about these fights was that they were always the same, she said, violent and embarrassing. Afterward, O.J. would become extremely contrite, and would buy something incredibly expensive by way of an apology. This time, she vowed to Kato, she wasn't going to accept any gifts, she wasn't going to forgive him. "I could be happy with someone else," she said. "I don't need O.J. Simpson." A little while later, as she sipped a hot cup of coffee, she said she wished she had someone real in her life.

Kato asked Nicole what had happened to provoke O.J. "into the kind of rage I'd never experienced before."

"Absolutely nothing," she said. "O.J.'s just . . . we're fighting again." She told Kato O.J. had come over a few nights earlier and had seen some photos of her and a man she used to date, on the den table. That had kicked off a new round of fights between them.

A while later Kato returned to his guest house, and had no sooner stepped inside than he got a phone call from an upset O.J. who wanted him "to come over for a while and talk."

"O.J. ," Kato said, "I don't know. Let me call you back."

He hung up and returned to the main house to check on Nicole. She seemed calmer now. Kato told her about O.J.'s phone call and she freaked out. "If you go over there," she cried, "I'll hate you. Don't you dare go over there!"

Kato was surprised. Although he should have expected that reaction, he hadn't. "Okay," he said. "But he really sounded upset on the phone."

"Kato," she said, on the edge of tears. "He's trying to manipulate you. Don't you see? I don't want you going over there."

"Okay," he said. "I won't. Should I call him back?"

"If you have to," Nicole said quietly.

Kato returned to the guest house and found another message flashing on his phone machine. He hit the button and listened. It was O.J. "Kato, call me if you're going to come by. I'm just here at home." He sounded more composed. Kato decided not to call.

Looking back on the incident, Kato recalled, "By the time I saw O.J. again, he and Nicole had made peace. The incident seemed completely forgotten by the both of them. At least, that's the way they acted, as if neither one wanted to admit it had ever taken place.

"Later on, when I began seeing O.J. more frequently, he did mention it to me one more time, although not in any apologetic or explanatory way. I don't remember how it came up, but he brushed it off, insisting it had been no big thing."

Late in December, Nicole, whom Kato described as "an easy touch, always giving money away," decided to cut her expenses by purchasing a small town house. The already high, $4,800-a-month rent at Gretna Green was about to jump to nearly $6,000. She'd finally been able to sell the condo in San Francisco and planned to use that money to purchase a place to live in.

She began actively searching for a house and, whenever possible, took Kato along. The first thing the kids would ask when they all looked at someplace new was, "Which room is Kato's?"

When Nicole thought she'd found the perfect spot, once again she decided to express her feelings to Kato indirectly. In a note she wrote she thought she'd found the right place, and hoped he was planning on moving with her. She promised that even though the place had a great gym and pool and tennis court, he could pay the same rent, and she would only let him move "when you find a wife—oh no!" She signed the note, "Love, me."

At the same time O.J. began talking about selling the Rockingham estate and moving Nicole and the kids to Florida. He loved it down there and wanted to make it his permanent base of operations. Among other things Florida had going for it—besides being in his opinion a great place to raise his children—was the distance between it and the Beverly Hills/Hollywood/Brentwood partytime axis he so often blamed for the failure of his marriage.

Nicole was ambivalent about the idea. One day she'd be all excited about it, say yes, she was going to do it, and the next she'd say no, she didn't want to move that far away from her family and friends.

Unsure of what to do about O.J., and needing to tighten her financial belt, Nicole went ahead and bought a town house on Bundy, in Brentwood, not very far from the house on Gretna Green and the Rockingham estate.

Just before she moved, O.J., Sydney, Justin, and Kato were invited to a Christmas party at Kris and Bruce Jenner's house on Mulholland Drive in the Hollywood Hills.

Earlier that day, a huge bouquet of flowers arrived at Rockingham for O.J. Nicole was there with the kids, and became quite upset by the delivery. She was convinced that Paula Barbieri had sent them, knowing Nicole would be there when they arrived. What especially rankled her was that she and O.J. were supposed to be in the middle of one of their many attempted reconciliations. This time O.J. promised, if things worked out, he would stop seeing Paula.

O.J. insisted he was innocent of any wrongdoing. He claimed he had no idea Paula was going to send him anything for Christmas. He told Nicole to look around at the hundreds of gifts that had arrived from agents, producers, former teammates, and friends. O.J. insisted that Paula's gift was nothing special.

Nicole, however, wasn't buying it. She maintained that Paula had done it on purpose, to ruin their holiday. It was on this note of conflict that they left for the party.

It became clear to Kato as soon as they arrived that there was a coolness between Jenner and O.J. Part of the reason, Kato believed, was that Kris Jenner had been married to Bob Kardashian before divorcing him to marry Bruce. In private, Kato knew, O.J. didn't have much use for Jenner and used to make fun of him, especially the stairstep machine "infomercial" he'd made. O.J. thought it was about the dumbest thing he'd ever seen, although he did have a lot of respect for the profit it turned.

Everyone else seemed in a great holiday mood, which lasted until Nicole and O.J. got into a fight over an ex-boyfriend of hers, Joseph Perulli, a good-looking model-actor type who happened to be at the party. His presence made O.J. furious. Worse, Nicole was friendly to Perulli.

It didn't take long for O.J. and Nicole to rev up the engines. After fifteen minutes of what turned out to be an extremely embarrassing shouting match, Nicole threw her hands up, smiled, went over to Kato, grabbed his arm, and said, almost comically, "Guess what, we're out of here! You can stay if you want to, it looks like it's going to be fun, but we're out of here! O.J. says we've got to go, so we've got to go!"

O.J., Nicole, the kids, and Kato all got back into the

Bentley. O.J. and Nicole sat in front, Kato and the kids in the rear. For the first couple of seconds there was total silence. Then O.J. started in. At the top of his voice, he shouted, *"You know, you blame me for these flowers that I get out of nowhere, that I had nothing to do with . . . and you go over and talk to that guy. . . ."*

"You're accusing me of what?" Nicole asked, adding that she wondered how he could have a problem with Joseph when he, O.J., was running around with a million women.

"I'm outraged you could even think such a thing!"

He continued to shout while Nicole said nothing. He somehow interpreted the incident as an attempt on Nicole's part to get revenge for a story that had just run in *The National Enquirer* about O.J. having other girlfriends. When it became apparent that he wasn't going to let up, she turned to him and said softly, "Please, please, O.J., let's not fight tonight, please, it's Christmas Eve. . . ."

Kato, meanwhile, tried to keep the kids occupied by opening some of the presents they'd gotten at the party.

But O.J. kept up. *"You don't believe me, do you?"* he shouted to her.

"I don't care. I don't care about believing you," Nicole said.

They finally arrived back at Rockingham, where Michelle, O.J.'s housekeeper, was preparing Christmas dinner. O.J. had invited all his relatives over. By the time everyone came together in the living room, the tension between O.J. and Nicole was thicker than the slabs of turkey laid out on the main platter.

Nicole decided she wasn't going to let O.J. ruin the holiday for the kids. She handed Kato a camcorder and told him to shoot scenes of her with the children, and of O.J. opening their gifts. O.J. handed his two older children, Jason and Arnelle, envelopes. Inside each were checks for $25,000. Merry Christmas. O.J. then opened his gift from Kato, a $12.98 Chia pet.

That caused a big laugh, which broke the tension. They all then dug into a fabulous dinner. Later on, O.J. gave Nicole an expensive diamond bracelet, and she gave him a silver picture frame. For the sake of the kids, they managed to put their differences aside for the remainder of the holiday evening.

**FROM THE TRIAL TESTIMONY OF BRIAN "KATO" KAELIN—
CALIFORNIA V. O.J. SIMPSON—MARCH 21, 1995
(Direct examination):**

Marcia Clark: Did you ever move into [the Bundy town house that Nicole purchased in January 1994] that you were going to?

Brian "Kato" Kaelin: No.

Marcia Clark: Why not?

Brian "Kato" Kaelin: I was going to move in and I moved in at O.J.'s.

Marcia Clark: Why not? Why did you do that?

Brian "Kato" Kaelin: Because O.J. asked me to go to his house. I mean, it was part of a deal. I went there instead of moving in with Nicole. There's—

Marcia Clark: What did the defendant say to you about moving into his house instead of Nicole's condominium, or town house?

Brian "Kato" Kaelin: I mean, we talked about it and it

was sort of like the right thing to do, not to be in the same house, that I should probably not go there, and O.J. offered me his place. It was free and he said you can stay as long as you want, and when it was time for you to go he'd let me know.

Marcia Clark: Did he indicate to you with respect to what he thought of the fact that you'd be living in the same house with Nicole?

Brian "Kato" Kaelin: Not—didn't like it, but it probably wouldn't be right.

Marcia Clark: And why wouldn't it be right?

Brian "Kato" Kaelin: I don't know the answer.

Kato maintains he had every intention of moving with Nicole and the kids to Bundy. It didn't happen, however, and his explanation to me differs from what he told the court, particularly as to O.J.'s motivations.

The day before Nicole was to take physical possession of the town house, Kato found himself wondering if this move was something he really wanted to do. The Bundy place was great, he could have his own room complete with a separate side entrance, but he'd begun to think about how maybe it was time to move on. The baby-sitting thing was starting to get a little old, and a smaller house would undoubtedly provide less privacy, less freedom.

Still, up until the very last minute, he had agreed to move with Nicole and the kids, at least for a little while.

He was packing his things in the guest house when he got a call from Nicole. She had just spoken to O.J. and said that

Kato was going to receive a call as well. She didn't say what the call was to be about.

A few minutes later the phone rang again and it was, indeed, O.J. "Listen, man," he said to Kato. "You're planning to move in with Nicole and the kids and all that, and I just want you to know how I feel about it."

"Okay," Kato said.

"It's up to you to do what you want, but I don't think it's right. As a man, Kato, I'm telling you I don't feel good about it. I don't think it's right for you to be living under the same roof as Nicole and the kids."

"I totally understand," Kato said. "And want to honor your request. The only problem is, I don't have anywhere else to go right now." He asked O.J. if it would be okay if he stayed with Nicole until he could find a place of his own.

"Kato," O.J. said, "you can move in with me. And you can stay as long as you want."

"Come on," Kato said, laughing at what he thought had to be a joke.

"I'm not kidding," O.J. said. "I have loads of room. You can have your own guest house. I'm serious."

"Well, even if I wanted to, I could never afford to live at your place."

"Hey, man, I don't want your money. I don't need it. You can stay for free."

Bingo.

The legendary Juice, rent-free estate, total access to his pool, his Jacuzzi, his world. A full-card win.

"Work things out with Nicole," O.J. said.

Kato thanked him and hung up the phone. He couldn't wait to tell Nicole "the good news." He went back to her house, found her in the kitchen, and told her about the phone call. "Guess what?" he said, "O.J. doesn't feel it's right for me to move in with you and the kids, and so he's offered to let me live in his guest house for free! Isn't that great?"

Nicole looked at him with an expression he'd never seen before. "He's manipulating you, Kato. Don't you see what he's trying to do?"

Kato claims he couldn't believe what he was hearing, and couldn't understand what she was so upset about. Apparently, the idea of betrayal never entered his mind. Instead, he tried to explain to her how perfect this seemed to him, but Nicole didn't want to hear any of it. She became extremely upset and cut short the discussion.

Kato went back to the guest house and started packing. A few minutes later Nicole came by to tell him she was sorry for blowing up, that she was okay with his moving in with O.J., and that she wasn't even angry with him for "doing this to us. Every time I make a friend, he takes them away from me."

"Nicole," Kato said, "he's not taking me away."

"You don't know him. He's manipulating you. He's not just taking you out of my house, he's taking you out of my life."

A while later Cora came by to see how the move was going. She and Kato talked, and he told her how bad he felt about what was going on. Cora said she understood, and thought that maybe part of the problem was that Nicole had been counting on his rent money.

He hadn't thought of that. He told Cora he would honor his commitment and move in with Nicole. He went down to the kitchen and told her of his new plan.

"No," Nicole, without emotion, said to the houseguest she had once declared with happiness and conviction she'd wanted to be friends with for the rest of her life. "It's okay. Go live with O.J."

5

Life with O.J.

FROM THE TRIAL TESTIMONY OF BRIAN "KATO" KAELIN—
CALIFORNIA V. O.J. SIMPSON—MARCH 27, 1995
(Redirect examination):

Marcia Clark: You stated an opinion that the defendant and Nicole had a good relationship for the time that you knew them. Do you recall that?

Brian "Kato" Kaelin: Yes.

———

"I love O.J., guilty or not guilty."

—*Brian "Kato" Kaelin,*
From an interview with
Marc Eliot, February 6, 1995

Brian "Kato" Kaelin moved

into O.J.'s Rockingham estate on January 7, the same day Nicole officially took possession of her new town house on Bundy.

In the days and weeks that followed, it became increasingly clear to Kato that Nicole was, in fact, quite angry with him, perhaps even a bit vindictive, and making a statement by keeping her distance, emotionally as well as physically.

To Nicole, the whole episode was just another example of O.J.'s need to control every aspect of her life. At the time, it was Kato's feeling that she saw him as some kind of trophy she'd lost and O.J. had won.

"I had never wanted there to be any change in our relationship just because I'd stopped living in her house," he said, "but she didn't see it that way. As a result, our friendship took a hit."

It started even before Kato left Gretna Green. Moving day was a bit of a mess, as both he and Nicole were busy getting their things together, loading up, and shipping out. Nicole had hired movers; Kato relied on his old friend Will Stumpe.

As Will and Kato finished their first fill-up of a rented van, Nicole stepped out her front door. "Hey," Kato said to Will, "there's Nicole. Come on, I'll introduce you." He waved at her, she saw him, got into her car, and drove away without saying a word. That was the moment Kato first realized just how angry and upset she really was.

Even with Will's help, the move proved to be an all-day job. They wound up making nearly twenty mile-and-a-half trips between Gretna Green and Rockingham. After they finished, Kato returned one last time to do a thorough clean-up and polish of the guest house.

When he arrived at Rockingham, Will had already moved a lot of his stuff into the guest house. As Kato began to help with the final load, O.J. passed by. He smiled and gave the two a thumbs up. Kato looked at him, grinned and shouted, "Roommates! Bachelors!" O.J. "cracked up laughing." That single gesture made Kato feel good, as if somehow confirming he had made the right decision.

"Kato," O.J. said, "you're going to be treated like King Farouk around here. You'll have food, the services of my maid Michelle, anything you want. All at your disposal."

As Kato was soon to discover, O.J. wasn't kidding. Everything he wanted *was* there for the asking. And sometimes he didn't even have to do that. For instance, there was always a lot of food in the house. Often, at night, Michelle would bring the day's leftovers to Kato in his room, and tell him he could eat as much as he wanted.

As for his feelings about "betraying" Nicole, Kato said, "I loved them both, and tried to interfere as little as possible in what was going on between them. If they were going to stay divorced, that was fine. I knew each of them would be able to move on and find new lives. If they were going to reconcile, that was great, too. I thought they made a great couple when they weren't fighting, and it would probably be good for the children as well.

"However, I'm not a marriage counselor. All I can say is I

honestly don't feel I was manipulated by O.J. into moving to his house.

"There was, and I won't deny it, a palpable shift in the way Nicole related to me. On the rare occasions I found myself at the Bundy residence, usually to deliver a package, or pick up the kids for O.J., I could feel the chill in the air. That was hard for me. I began to feel like a pawn between the two enclaves, some kind of bizarre go-between on the rough road between Rockingham Way and Bundy Drive."

O.J. was constantly on the go, and at first, most of the time he and Kato saw each other was either to wave hello or good-bye, as The Juice seemed always to be just arriving from or about to leave on a trip.

Kato kept busy as well, devoting more and more of his time to Alan and Diane Mehrez's film company, trying to learn as much about the business as he could. He had, in fact, advanced to the point where Diane felt she could hire him as her full-time assistant.

One of the first things O.J. and Kato actually did together, not very long after Kato moved in, was to watch a play-off game one Sunday that January between the Detroit Lions and the Green Bay Packers. Having grown up in Wisconsin, Kato is a lifelong Green Bay fan.

Kato had originally planned to watch the game in his room, and asked O.J. if he minded Will coming over. O.J. looked at him like he was crazy, frowned, then smiled and said, "What's the matter with you? Of course you can have a friend come by! You don't have to ask me that."

In fact, the reason Kato felt he did have to ask had nothing really to do with O.J. Since the first day Kato had moved in, the football legend had gone out of his way to make him feel at home. It was O.J.'s maid Michelle who seemed determined to make Kato feel as unwelcome as possible.

Whenever anybody came by to visit the new houseguest, even if for only a little while, at some point Michelle would take Kato aside and whisper, "O.J.'s not going to like this!" Kato recalled, "At times she reminded me more of a dictator than a housekeeper. I began to think of her as the Absolute Monarch of Rockingham."

Michelle is a veteran of the Israeli army, and, according to Kato, "absolutely anal" about O.J. and his home, the type who wiped a table where a coffee cup sat whenever you picked it up to take a sip.

The Northridge earthquake of January 17, 1994, happened about a week after Kato's move. That night he happened to be working late on the set of a film. When the quake hit, he had just pulled into Diane Mehrez's driveway, gotten out of his car, and gone into the living room, hoping to catch some sleep on the couch. He had decided to stay there instead of going back to O.J.'s because of the lateness of the hour, and because Diane had agreed to watch Kato's daughter, Tiffany, whom he had for the weekend and who liked staying at Diane's and playing with her children. Whenever possible, Kato liked to be there in the morning when Tiffany woke up.

After the quake struck, the first thing Kato did was to make sure everyone in the house was all right. Fortunately, no one was hurt, and structural damage was minimal.

Early the next morning, Kato drove to O.J.'s to see if *his* house was still standing. As it happened, O.J. was out of town, which meant that Michelle was left in charge. Except for some trophies that had fallen over, and some minor damage, O.J., too, got off pretty easy.

However, Kato hadn't bothered to tell Michelle he wouldn't be sleeping in the guest house the night before. His schedule was always unstructured, and most of the time he never knew where he was going to be. He hadn't realized that when Michelle checked out the house and didn't find him, she would fear that he was buried underneath a pile of as-yet-undiscovered rubble.

When Kato drove up and Michelle saw that he wasn't hurt, her attitude shifted. No longer concerned for his safety, she seemed angry, until she began to joke about how Kato hadn't been there when he was actually needed for something—to protect her when the quake had struck.

A day or so later, when O.J. returned, he asked Michelle to do an inventory check. He wanted to know what things of his had been damaged or broken. That's when she first noticed that something was askew.

She had the layout of O.J.'s trophy room memorized, and was able to tell whenever anything was even a little out of place. After making a thorough inspection, she proudly announced to O.J. that a trophy from his collection was missing. Moreover, she thought one of the construction workers might have taken it. Although she seemed outraged, O.J. decided not to pursue the matter.

That Sunday, as planned, Will came over to watch the Green Bay game. During the first quarter, O.J. came by the guest house and invited both Kato and Will to watch the rest of it with him in the main house on the projection TV. The picture and sound were so realistic, Kato thought, "it was like having a seat on the fifty-yard line."

As Kato settled in and made himself comfortable, out of the corner of his eye he could see Michelle shaking her head disapprovingly.

O.J. said the beer was in the bar fridge and the boys should help themselves. At first, he had no idea that Kato, and Will, too, were such intense Green Bay Packer fans. When he realized, he started regaling them with stories about his playing days at USC, during which time his quarterback had been Mike Holmgren, who was now the coach of Green Bay.

"Yeah, I remember Holmgren," O.J. drawled. "His big play was always the same, handing off the ball to me. I'd run for a touchdown, and after, Mike would say, 'Hey, I'm doing good!' I'd grin and tell him, 'I think I'm doing all the work!'"

Once O.J. started reminiscing, there was no stopping him. It was as if he hadn't had anyone to sit around and schmooze about those days with for years. It became clear to Kato early on that O.J. never threw parties, or had a lot of people over. This was as much an opportunity for O.J. to "hang with his homies" as it was for Kato and Will to watch the game with The Juice.

Every once in a while O.J. would get up to go to the bathroom or get another beer. During these brief absences, Will would turn to Kato and say, "Does he realize we're trying to watch the game?" Then they'd both "crack up."

When Green Bay pulled off a dramatic win in the last second, Kato and Will jumped up and gave each other twenty high-fives, which really made O.J. laugh. He couldn't believe how much they were into it. "Next week," he said, "you guys play Dallas. That'll be some game." He invited Kato and Will to come back and watch the game with him.

As it turned out, O.J. couldn't watch that game because he had to prepare for a meeting scheduled later that afternoon with Skip Taft, his business attorney. However, he insisted the two watch it on the big-screen TV anyway.

Periodically, Michelle would come by to check on them. They happened to be eating pretzels, and every time a crumb would fall she'd silently point to it, and Kato would go diving.

At halftime, she informed them that they were to go back to Kato's room to watch the rest of the game, because O.J. had this very important meeting in the living room and they would be interfering with it. Just then, O.J. happened to walk by and asked why they were leaving. Kato told him what Michelle said, and O.J. shook his head and laughed. "She's too much! Don't pay any attention to her, fellas. Relax and enjoy the game."

Not only that, but he insisted that Kato stay for the meeting. "There's a merchandising deal I'm considering, and would like to know what you think." O.J. was considering investing in wristwatches from Russia, to be sold in America. The recent breakup of the Soviet Union had created a wave of "Russiamania" in the States, and O.J. sensed an opportunity to make a killing. A group of business partners was coming over to show him a sample, and he wanted Kato's input.

During the meeting he turned to Kato and said, "What do you think of these watches?"

Kato said, "Well, comrade, I think they're great, and will probably sell a lot."

According to Kato, "He shook his head. I couldn't believe it. O.J. was treating me not only as a friend, but someone whose opinion he respected. Man, I thought to myself, this is one super-cool dude.

"I have to say that right up until the end, O.J. continued to include me in these kind of things. The week before the murders, O.J. had Paula Barbieri over for dinner and invited me as well because later that evening, Steve Sabol, the owner of NFL films, was going to be coming by, along with a film crew, to shoot an interview. I was like, how cool is this! Dinner with O.J. *and* the legendary Steve Sabol. I loved it!"

With every day that went by, Kato said, he felt more and more welcome in O.J.'s house. "Juiceage," as Kato called him, loved to sit around, have a beer, and talk about his "glory" days playing football for USC and Buffalo, and he, Kato, loved to listen. "We were like a couple of college roomies."

And like "college roomies," O.J. loved to joke around. He always seemed to be calling Kato over to share a funny line, or an observation that had made him laugh. Most of the time he'd say something, chuckle, then Kato would say something and O.J. would double up.

Kato soon discovered that when O.J. was home for any length of time, his idea of spending a perfect afternoon was sitting in front of the big-screen TV, channel-surfing and making jokes about what was on. He had the latest TV satellite system so he could follow what was one of his true passions, televised sports. On Sundays, he'd have three sets up in the living room, the big screen and two smaller screens on either side, which allowed him to watch several games at the same time.

O.J. was also quite passionate about his music collection. According to Kato, he had a great set of records, tapes, and CDs. He was into jazz, Frank Sinatra, and big-band music. And he was a perfectionist when it came to the latest stereo equipment. Kato recalled one time O.J. purchased an expensive new set of speakers and couldn't get one of them to sound just the way he wanted. He wound up working on it all day, going over the wiring, the placement, the connections, with all the concentration of a brain surgeon.

The more Kato got to know O.J., the more he felt able to kid him about how "white" he was. O.J. didn't drink, he didn't stay up late, he woke up at the crack of dawn, he didn't like to dance, he couldn't sing, he didn't listen to rap music, and he wasn't into drugs. Kato liked to kid O.J. by telling him he was the whitest black man who'd ever lived. O.J. got a kick out of jokes like that.

Golf was another passion of O.J.'s. He played golf every day his schedule permitted, often getting up at five in the morning to avoid the crowds.

People were always coming by the house for pictures and autographs, and he was always very good about it. He liked giving out his autograph, and arranging perks for friends. However, there were times when it became a little too much for him, especially when the life of the legend intersected too closely with the life of the man.

One time Cora Fischman came by with four or five footballs she wanted signed for some friends of hers. This was a particularly busy time for O.J., and he didn't get to them right away. She began to press him, and he blew up; not immdiately, but after he'd spoken to her on the phone. O.J. and Nicole had had an argument the night before, and for some reason, he believed Cora had instigated it. Eventually, he found out he was wrong, but he never signed the footballs.

O.J.'s friends and business associates were constantly coming by, and sometimes stayed the night.

Ron Shipp was an ex-cop who used to visit the house quite often with friends to play tennis. Sometimes Ron would be on the tennis courts with three friends, and O.J. nowhere in sight. "He was always friendly to me," Kato said, "but I know his hanging around bothered O.J." Toward the end, whenever Shipp would show up, O.J. would look at Kato, raise his eyes to the sky, and say, "Oh no, Ron's here again. I need to talk to him about this."

Shipp got to know the ins and outs of the house. He discovered, for example, that the Ashford gate had a latch that could be opened from the outside. Kato often used it to let himself in when he'd come home late. He preferred using this method because the Rockingham gate worked electronically and had a slow, lumbering motion, which meant having to wait until it completely opened, and then completely shut. On a cold night, with O.J.'s dog barking at his feet, it wasn't the most pleasant way to pass five or ten minutes.

A.C. Cowlings lived nearby and came over all the time. Whenever he'd see Kato he'd say, "Hey, man, how're you doin'?" Michelle would always be happy to see him and the first thing she'd do was make him something to eat.

After he'd leave, Michelle would tell Kato stories about how much A.C. owed O.J., how O.J. had helped A.C. get off "crack," and back on "the straight and narrow." She said that there was a time when A.C. used to come over and hang around watching TV all day. It drove O.J. crazy, she said, until finally he had a long a talk with A.C. about it. Certain rules of visitation were laid out, and A.C. never broke them. He also stopped coming by as often.

When Kato realized how many times guests slept over, he told O.J. if he ever needed to use the guest room, he (Kato) could always stay with a friend for a night or two. O.J. told him to forget it; he lived there and shouldn't concern himself with such things.

"Still," Kato said later, "whenever Michelle caught me alone for a minute, she would take me by the arm and whisper in my ear, 'Did you find a place yet? When are you moving out?'"

One time he reminded her what O.J. had promised when he'd moved in, that he could stay as long as he wanted to. "No," she insisted, "he wants you to leave. He asked me to find out exactly when you're moving out."

"God," Kato thought, "I can't believe it. Okay . . . I'll pack up my stuff and try to find a place." Before he actually did anything, though, he decided to talk to O.J. and apologize for overstaying his welcome.

O.J. told him to stop worrying, that he didn't have to move. "When I want you out of this place," he told Kato, "*I'll* tell you, not Michelle." At that point, Kato volunteered to pay some rent, which made O.J. laugh. "I don't want your money, that's got nothing to do with anything."

O.J. decided to have a talk with Michelle, but it didn't help.

She still kept after Kato, day after day, coming into his room and telling him it would be a good idea if he moved out. "Have you found a place yet?" she'd ask. Now, though, Kato had what he thought was the perfect answer. "No, but I'm looking," he'd reply.

Kato felt as if he'd made a new, terrific friend in O.J. Simpson. "Juiceage" told him he could hang out in the main house anytime he wanted.

"I thought that was really great of him, but never took advantage of the privilege," Kato told me. "I almost never went there unless specifically invited.

Kato got a charge out of watching O.J. eat breakfast—carrot juice, toast, eggs, and jelly. He enjoyed the spectacle of O.J. inhaling one portion after the other, fast and methodically, like a highly efficient machine.

However, because O.J. used to get up early to play golf, Kato, who is not a morning person, would often have breakfast alone, or with Michelle occasionally joining him for a cup of coffee. If she wasn't after him to move out, she'd go on about what Kato soon discovered was her second favorite topic.

Nicole.

Michelle hated her, and whenever she got the opportunity, would go on about what an awful woman she thought she was.

"Nicole is no good," she'd tell Kato. "She can't cook like I can for him. She ought to be grateful to have the opportunity to be by his side." Kato would just shake his head and say nothing, letting her rattle on.

O.J. volunteered to help Kato out with his career. He made lots of phone calls to friends in the film business to tell them they should check him out to see if he wasn't right for this part or that.

And Kato wasn't the only one he tried to help. At the time O.J. was working for Kushner-Locke on an HBO series called *First and Ten*, in which he played the show's "stud." He made several calls trying to get Marcus Allen a shot on the show.

"After a while O.J. began to open up to me," Kato recounted, "and we'd have long talks about lots of things, including, most often, his relationship with Nicole." O.J.'s obsessing about her was most often triggered by an incident that upset him. For instance, O.J. would invite Nicole to go on a trip with him, she'd agree, and to help out her family, he'd have his assistant Cathy book the tickets through her mother Juditha Brown's travel agency.

When Nicole would cancel at the last minute, it would drive O.J. crazy.

He hated the fact that she changed her mind, and usually at the last possible moment. This would cause him to stew for a few days, and then he'd start talking to Kato about how he knew that all of Nicole's problems stemmed from the fact that she was a part of "the Master Race."

O.J. had a theory about why they had such trouble getting along. He said it was because of her heritage. "It's that German thing," he would say to Kato. "It's in her genes."

O.J. would then shift to Nicole's "drinking problem," how that was the cause of her many mood swings. Kato agreed that Nicole's mood could and often did shift from one extreme to another, sometimes on a daily basis. She could be extremely up one day and markedly sullen the next.

O.J. was convinced that Nicole's drinking was going to lead to liver failure. "She drinks so much tequila," he'd say to Kato, "she doesn't realize that's going to hurt her. It's already starting to show on her skin. And it makes her a mean person. She's mean, you know." He also complained about her smoking and how she seemed to do nothing all day but waste time. "She has no activities, no life," he'd say. "She has nothing to keep her busy."

This line would usually lead to his complaining about her circle of girlfriends, how he didn't think they were "good" for her, especially Faye Resnick, whom he singled out. He was convinced Faye was a "bad influence" on Nicole and was leading her down the wrong path. There were rumors afloat in their circle that Faye was trying to lure Nicole into the world of lesbianism (and, supposedly, three-way sex), and it bothered O.J. To a man whose identity was so defined by maleness, the thought of his wife being taken away by a woman must have seemed intolerable. It was a specially tight turn of a very unpleasant screw.

Kato didn't think it helped matters any that Faye was constantly after O.J. to introduce her to Paula. Faye said she wanted to be friends with everybody. O.J. never did make this introduction.

During one of their attempts at reconciliation, Nicole wanted to find something new she could share with O.J. Because he loved golf so much, she decided to try to learn how to play and, for a while, accompanied him to the various country clubs to which he belonged.

O.J. loved this, to the point where, at Nicole's urging, he even agreed to let Cici come along one time. After Faye, Cici was O.J.'s least favorite of Nicole's friends. He told Kato later that all during the game, Cici talked nonstop about her problems with men, which, O.J. said, made Nicole a little uneasy. "After all," he said, "here we are trying to reconcile."

At one point, he told Kato, Nicole turned to Cici and said, "Why don't you just drop it!" The two women then got into a big fight, right there on the green, which, O.J. said cracked him up. "It was so great," he said, "a real catfight."

243

According to Kato, O.J. used to joke about Cici all the time. "How old is that woman," he'd say, grinning, "ninety-three? No wonder she's so sour. What man would want to be with her?"

He also talked at length to Kato about his relationship with Paula Barbieri. He said Paula lived in fear that he would one day get back together with Nicole. Paula, he claimed, wanted desperately to marry him, but knew that no matter how close they got, there would always be the specter of Nicole.

O.J. and Paula took trips all the time. They went to Miami, Palm Springs, New York, and O.J. loved being seen with her. However, unlike his behavior with Nicole, he wasn't overly possessive. One of the reasons, perhaps, is because he really didn't love her. Or at least feel about her the way he did about Nicole, for which *love* might not be the best word.

"One time," Kato said, "he told me that Paula had expressed a desire to have children with him, and he said in no uncertain terms that he didn't want any more kids.

"'Kato,' he said, 'I *got* kids. Four kids. What do I want any more for? I got dogs, I got kids, I'm done with that part of my life.'"

It became a major issue between O.J. and Paula, one over which he refused to compromise.

O.J. told Kato he was worried about what he referred to only as "some KKK group." He believed "they" were out to get him. Several times during the months Kato lived at his house he told him about a group he knew of that hated blacks and Jews, and because he was black and an active fund-raiser for several Jewish charitable organizations, he was the top target on their hit list. He was convinced his life was in danger, and that "they" wouldn't rest until he was dead. He told Kato he had heard about this from several of his detective friends and that the FBI had also been in contact to warn him.

As a result, he said, he was constantly in fear of "being hit." He said he'd told Nicole about it, but that she didn't believe him.

All the time that Kato lived at Rockingham, O.J. seemed determined to win Nicole back and was willing to try anything. He arranged for her to receive bouquets of flowers every week. Although he never enjoyed this type of thing, he would occasionally offer to take Nicole out for a night on the town. He did it, he told Kato, mainly to prove he wasn't too old to have a good time.

He often complained to Kato that she was forever reminding him of the fourteen-year age difference between them, that he was getting older, that she didn't look forward to one day living with an arthritic man she'd have to push around in a wheelchair. And she'd taunt him about his body by poking him in the stomach to point out the "little pot" he was developing.

He liked to take Nicole out for dinner to a restaurant where they could spend a quiet evening, then return right home, while Nicole preferred to go clubbing and stay out all night. That would make him angry. "Doesn't she understand," he would say to Kato, "I get up at six in the morning! I have a million things to take care of! By the end of the day I'm exhausted! The last thing in the world I want to do is go out and party all night!"

The first time Kato saw Nicole after moving out of Gretna Green was about a month later, when he'd settled comfortably into Rockingham. Nicole had come over to spend the night with O.J. This wasn't that unusual an occurrence. Sometimes Kato would come home, decide to grab a bite to eat in the kitchen, and discover O.J. and Nicole and all the kids up in the bedroom watching TV, like the happiest, most together family that ever lived.

According to Kato, this night, she was polite but unmistakably cool toward him. They talked a little, but really didn't say very much to each other.

The next morning, at breakfast, O.J. told Kato what a great time he'd had. Kato later said he remembered catching a glimpse of Nicole at that moment and seeing a hurt look cross her face as O.J. shared this private moment with his houseguest.

"It wasn't only that he had told me something intimate between the two of them, but I sensed a bit of jealousy on her part at how close O.J. and I had become. I wondered if maybe she had begun to redirect some of her anger at O.J. toward me."

That thought troubled Kato for a while. After all, Nicole had been a good friend and he wanted her to know it.

He decided to write Nicole a long letter to express his positive feelings and assure her he hoped they would be friends until the day they died. To underscore his feelings, he included a tape of songs to convey his sincerity. A few days later she called to thank him for the letter and the tape, but she made her coolness toward him apparent. "Yeah," she said on the phone, "I got the letter and the tape. It doesn't make me feel any better."

Kato still ran into Nicole during his morning runs along the San Vicente jogging route. Because he is a long-distance runner, he tends to become intensely focused and somewhat inner-directed. One morning, after doing his ten miles, he came back to O.J.'s and found Nicole and Cora working out in the garage. They had both gotten into weight training, and O.J. had offered to let them use his equipment. When Nicole saw Kato, she asked why he hadn't said hello earlier that day while running. "I explained that I didn't see her, but I could tell she didn't believe me. When I tried to reassure her that I would never not say hello to her, she said okay, and brushed me off. I felt terrible."

Nicole often came by O.J.'s to lie out in the sun by the pool. One time, during an attempted reconciliation period, Kato happened to have his daughter visiting for the weekend. Sydney was with Nicole by the pool. Kato decided to go over and say hello. Nicole asked him when he was planning to move out. "I felt bad," Kato told me, "because Tiffany and Sydney were friends, and they had no idea they might not be able to stay friends because of the ongoing tension between Nicole and me."

Another time a director friend of Kato's was over, and they were playing tennis on O.J.'s court. Later that day O.J. took Kato aside and told him Nicole had asked when he was leaving, and said Kato had to go before there could be any reconciliation between her and O.J. Kato claims he volunteered to pack his bags that day, but before he did, O.J. told him not to worry, wink wink, he had no intention of asking him to leave, that he liked having him around and wanted him to stay.

O.J. often went to Nicole's new place on Bundy to visit and would occasionally stay the night.

There were several trips they were supposed to take together that winter and spring, which Nicole bowed out of at the last minute. Miami, New York, Cabo San Lucas. Sometimes he'd go by himself, and no one would have any idea where he was, or for how long. He'd just be gone, until he'd reappear.

According to Kato, "There were times I thought Nicole was purposely trying to drive him crazy. I couldn't understand why she would agree to go away with him if she had no intention of actually making the trip. The thought of being with her used to really bring him up, and the letdown when she told him she wasn't going would send him crashing. They'd fight, she'd warn him that she wasn't going to let him in her life again, then they'd make up, and they'd be all lovey-dovey. Until the next fight."

Although O.J. often talked about wanting to reconcile with Nicole, he was involved with Paula throughout the time Kato lived at his house. Kato didn't actually spend any real time with Paula until early in May. Still, he'd heard a lot about her from O.J. "One of the things I remember he liked," Kato recalled, "was the resemblance between Paula and Julia Roberts, which, he told me, always made her furious."

One Sunday O.J. took Kato to a Raiders/Browns football game, during which he told him a story about how when he and Paula were out one evening a valet said to them, "Mr. Simpson? Ms. Roberts? Your car is ready."

She got really angry, O.J. said, because he had gone along with the valet, pretending that Paula *was* Julia Roberts! Just to get her going sometimes O.J. even called her Julia. Then he'd laugh hysterically when she'd get offended. He could never understand why. He thought it was a great compliment for any woman to be mistaken for Julia Roberts.

It was great fun for Kato to go to a football game with O.J. He'd get to hang with him everywhere, in the press room, the food room, down on the sidelines. When O.J. did his commentary for NBC, Kato was right there alongside him, just out of camera range.

During one game, O.J. boasted that one of the Raiderette cheerleaders was coming on to him. She was a beautiful blonde. Not long after that Sunday, she started making regular visits to the house.

"One time," Kato said, "I ran into her coming through the gate as I was heading out. The next day O.J. told me she said I was a really nice-looking guy. O.J. then pretended she had to be out of her mind to think such a thing. It was O.J.'s way of sharing this little adventure with me."

There were always plenty of women in O.J.'s life. Some of them were involved with other people. At least one Kato knew of was married. O.J. didn't think much of any of them. They were groupies, as far as he was concerned. The married one bothered him, because he liked her husband, but none meant anything more to him than a "quick pop." They were purely sexual relationships, and he saw no contradiction between his involvement, such as it was, with any of them, and his ongoing desire to reconcile with Nicole. After all, he was divorced, good-looking, wealthy, charming, and sexual. "A stud," as Kato described him.

"If I had any second thoughts," Kato recalled, "it was to question how much he was really into Nicole. If it were me, and I was trying to reconcile with my ex-wife, I wouldn't have my social calendar as full as he kept his and would concentrate my efforts more on getting back together. However, it wasn't me, and I wasn't about to tell O.J. how to live his life, or judge his actions."

Sometimes O.J. would take Kato into the den, pull out pictures of beautiful women he had dated, or was dating, and show them off.

Michelle would occasionally come in to see if they needed anything, and O.J. would quickly hide the photos, as if they were something he didn't want her to know about. She'd leave, he'd laugh, and then pull them back out.

Of course, Michelle knew everything about O.J.'s women. Whenever the occasion arose, she'd take Kato aside and whisper to him that O.J. "had a friend staying the night."

249

One time O.J. told Kato how he'd brought a girl to the house when he and Nicole were still married, and had sex with her. That was "the old O.J.," he said, "the one that did crazy things. Nicole was right here in the living room and I'd snuck this girl into the guest house. Nicole caught me, and boy, was she mad! But like I say, that was the old O.J. I would never do anything like that now."

Other times O.J. would point a girl out in a magazine and tell Kato when and how he'd had her. And there were women, he told Kato, who liked to do strange things for him. Women who "liked to eat each other's pussies" and wanted him to watch.

Nor did O.J. make any attempt to keep secret his relationship with Paula. He allowed himself to be photographed with her everywhere and openly brought her into his circle of friends. Nicole knew about her and liked her. With rare exception (the Christmas flowers incident, for example) she didn't appear jealous, or seem to mind O.J.'s involvement with Paula, especially when she found out how much she liked the kids. It's possible Nicole was hoping O.J. would marry Paula, which would then free her to start a new life. Not that she had put it completely on hold. She had her share of boyfriends as well all during their so-called attempts at reconciling.

The winter Kato lived at Rockingham, O.J.'s professional plate was full. He was involved in several major projects, including the pilot he was shooting in which he was to play a Navy SEAL. O.J. was particularly excited about this series, because for the first time in quite a while he had the opportunity to play a dramatic action character rather than a stud or buffoon.

One day after he completed filming, O.J. asked if Kato would like to see a tape of some of the footage. Kato said sure, and O.J. put it on. Afterward, he asked Kato what he thought of it, and Kato said how much he liked it. O.J. shook his head up and down, as excited as Kato had ever seen him.

He was also involved in a number of promos and commercial endorsements, traveling around the country making personal appearances and giving lectures for a new product he was marketing called "Juice Plus," a "wonder drug" for the treatment of arthritis. He also made a workout video, in which he arranged for Kato to make an appearance.

It sometimes felt to Kato as if O.J. kept his days so full in order not to have to face the two things that made him crazy, boredom and loneliness, the latter even worse with Nicole and the kids gone. "Why am I living here alone like this, Kato?" he'd ask during their talks. "I should sell everything and move to Florida. I don't need this big house. I can always fly in to L.A. and stay in a hotel when I have to and take care of business. I don't like living here anymore. I should just up and take Nicole and the kids and leave."

However, Kato believed there was another reason O.J. liked Florida so much. He had a friend down there who was a talent agent and a bit of a ladies' man. Every so often he would introduce O.J. to starlets. There was one, a gorgeous blonde, whom O.J. really liked. He used to call all the time and ask if she wanted him to come and visit. She rarely said no.

As the winter progressed, O.J. talked to Kato with increasing frequency about his repeatedly frustrated attempts at reconciling with Nicole. He'd make that face that has become so familiar to the world during the trial—squeezing his lips together and frowning while shaking his head back and forth—and try to figure out what he was doing wrong.

In March, O.J. was invited to an Academy Award party at Roxbury, one of the most sought-after Hollywood invitations of the year. He invited Nicole, and she turned him down. The night of the party he got dressed, got into his car, drove off, and returned a few minutes later, telling Kato he just didn't feel like going by himself.

O.J. would often come up with reasons for not being able to effect a full reconciliation that had nothing to do with his actual relationship with Nicole. For instance, O.J. said he knew she and the kids hated Michelle, and believed that this was one of the reasons Nicole wouldn't get back together with him.

In truth, the bad blood between Nicole and Michelle had been brewing for a long time. One of the conditions Nicole had laid down for a reconciliation was that O.J. had to fire Michelle, in spite of the fact that she'd been with him for eighteen years. If Michelle was there, Nicole told O.J., she would never move back in.

Whatever Michelle's motivations, she really had no use for Nicole. Things came to a head one Saturday when the kids came by Rockingham to go swimming. They brought Kato the dog with them, the Akita O.J. had given Nicole and the kids, who'd named him after their favorite houseguest ("it used to be a little confusing at Gretna Green, because I was never sure if the kids or Nicole were calling me or the dog").

Kato the dog had been playing with the kids, gotten his paws wet, then went bounding into the kitchen. Michelle threw a fit and screamed at Sydney and Justin. Nicole became incensed and told Michelle she was never to yell at the children. Heated words were exchanged, resulting in Nicole's hauling off and slapping Michelle hard across her face. "I hope you die!" Michelle screamed as she ran from the room in tears.

She wore Nicole's handprint on her cheek that night, which turned a deep dark purple and lasted for several days. She was determined to sue Nicole and had gone so far as to see a lawyer. O.J. decided to stay out of it. He knew that Nicole had struck Michelle and figured he had no right to prevent his maid from taking legal action. It went right up to setting a court date before Michelle dropped it, fearing the story would hit the tabloids and somehow hurt O.J.'s image.

Not long after, she resigned.

O.J. used to throw a party every spring for the Sunshine School, where Justin was enrolled. This year, both O.J. and Nicole were compatible enough to serve as co-hosts. They were expecting hundreds of people at Rockingham. To accommodate everyone, O.J. decided to move all the lawn furniture out of the way.

At one point Nicole asked Kato to help and he said he'd be happy to. It was one of the few times since he'd moved in with O.J. that she seemed completely friendly to him. It was a very important function for her; Kato knew it and was eager to help make it a success in any way he could. He also hoped it meant the beginning of a thaw in their friendship.

Unfortunately, Nicole ended up leaving early, because of yet another disagreement with O.J. over who-knows-what.

In April, O.J. and Nicole flew to Cabo. During the trip O.J. became convinced they were going to be able to get back together for good. He went so far as to tell Nicole he would end his relationship with Paula. He was going to buy a beautiful piece of beachfront property and build a dream house for the whole family to live in and enjoy. He even had blueprints drawn up and showed them to Nicole. At first she encouraged O.J. to go ahead and build the house. The next day, according to Kato, she changed her mind and told him to "forget it."

Originally it was supposed to be just the two of them, but before they left, Faye Resnick was somehow invited. By the time they actually departed, the group had grown to nearly a dozen, including kids.

Still, O.J. and Nicole got along really well, until he had to leave early to shoot additional scenes for his Navy-SEAL TV pilot. When she returned, Nicole told Kato she'd had a great time, but still wasn't sure things could work out. The morning after O.J. left, some new guy she'd seen on the beach had caught her fancy.

And there was still the Kato "problem." Nicole kept insisting he had to move out before she would move back in. However, before Kato even began to look for a place, the reconciliation fell apart. It broke down this time in May, when O.J. gave Nicole the platinum bracelet (the one he would eventually give to Paula).

The next day O.J. told Kato he didn't have to worry about moving anymore, because it was all over for good between Nicole and him.

The day after that they were back on.

Kato didn't understand what was going on. The whole thing seemed like one long soap opera, full of melodramatic behavior with nothing ever really happening. His attitude was if it was going to work between them, great, if not, also great, because then he and O.J. could go out and party. "I tried to be supportive of O.J., no matter what," Kato insisted.

Whatever had caused the latest split between Nicole and O.J., it seemed more serious than their previous breakups. Nicole was so angry that when O.J. would come by her place to pick up the kids, she'd leave everything outside her front door. Including the kids.

Later on, if they'd left anything behind, like a video game, she'd come by his house and leave it outside his front door. She didn't want any contact with him at all.

Nicole wasn't the only one causing O.J. problems. While he was living in the guest house, Kato couldn't help but be aware of the sometimes intense discussions O.J. used to get into with Arnelle. He didn't like the fact that she didn't have a steady job, or any particular career goals. He wanted her to focus on something, anything, and was terribly frustrated when she continued to concentrate mostly on partying.

Worse, before she left O.J.'s employ, Michelle would keep tabs on all the alcohol in the house, going so far as to mark the levels of the bottles. She would then report to O.J. how much was missing and usually blame Arnelle. Time and again he would complain about how his daughter would sleep in until one in the afternoon, then get ready to party.

Eventually, O.J. set Arnelle up with a job in wardrobe at one of the studios. She became pretty good at it, and started getting a lot of work, including several music videos. She even managed to land a onetime gig as a backup singer on the *Arsenio Hall Show.*

She also began dating Shaquille O'Neal, which O.J. liked. "Shacking with Shaq," as Kato put it. O.J. kept telling Arnelle to pursue a relationship. "That boy's got a lot of money," he'd say, and laugh.

As for Jason, he didn't come by all that often. When he did, it was usually with his girlfriend to go swimming. Jason was a professional chef. According to Kato, "There were a lot of things about him that weren't so great; he liked to fight a lot and had some legal problems himself, but O.J. overlooked them because Jason seemed focused on his career, especially after he managed to land the chef's position at broadcaster Michael Jackson's restaurant. At the Memorial Day party Jason and Arnelle threw, he did all of the cooking, and it was terrific."

According to Kato, Jason and Arnelle occasionally took Sydney and Justin to the movies, but basically, the two sets of kids didn't have much to do with each other. There was a definite feeling that these were two separate generations of Simpsons, and the older ones wanted to keep it that way.

As if things couldn't be any worse between O.J. and Nicole, in late May there were rumors in the Rockingham air that Faye was leading Nicole down some very dark alleys. Faye, word had it, wanted to become sexually involved with Nicole. "And from what I understood," Kato recalled, "Nicole liked it. At least the excitement of the experiment."

Whenever Nicole had an evening of lovemaking planned at the Gretna Green house, she would light candles in the living room and the bedroom. It was almost ritualistic, as if the candlelight held some mystical power to enhance the evening.

A very close friend of Nicole's told Kato that Nicole wanted to try three-way sex, two women and a man and she was looking for "candidates," one of whom, but neither the first nor only man considered, was Ron Goldman.

Nicole knew Ron from Mezzaluna; they belonged to the same health club, The Gym on San Vicente. He had driven her car several times and she had tried to help him out by making a few phones calls on his behalf to friends of hers in the film industry.

One of the things that bothered Kato about the night of the murders is that police found lit candles throughout Nicole's town house, and that her body was discovered wearing the same black dress she'd worn to the recital.

"I don't know if Nicole was expecting Ron," Kato told me, "or if she was expecting someone else, if she was holding 'auditions,' or if he even had any idea about the so-called plan. I do know that on June 12, Faye was in rehab, so no three-way, at least not with her, not that night. However, those candles, and the presence of Ron Goldman, continue to haunt me."

———

Sometime during the first week of June, O.J. and Kato were driving in the Bronco, returning home from one event or another. He and Nicole were supposed to have gone to a friend's wedding in Florida, but the trip was called off because of the current "down" state of their relationship. As a result, O.J.'s social calendar had a lot of openings.

Earlier that week, O.J. told Kato about a sports extravaganza scheduled to take place at the Century Plaza Hotel in Los Angeles. During this conversation he asked Kato what he was doing on July 4th. Kato said he had no plans and O.J. asked if he'd be his guest at the event. Kato said he'd love to and told him how much he appreciated his thinking of him.

"I remember he was in that zone he used to get into," Kato told me, "where he'd become very quiet and stare off into space, deep in thought. I was always amazed he could actually drive that way without crashing into a brick wall."

O.J. pulled up to his entrance gate on Ashford and for a few seconds they sat there in silence. Finally, Kato said, "Juice, I'd love to be you."

He turned to me and said, "Kato, you don't want to be me. You don't want to be me at all."

That July 4th, neither Kato nor O.J. attended the sports show at Century City. Both would have an unbreakable prior commitment to appear at Simpson's preliminary hearing.

By early June, Kato claims he was actively looking for a place to move. He says he was set up by June 1, in a place in San Vicente, when, at the last minute, the person who'd promised him the apartment gave it to someone else.

———

On June 5, the Sunday before the murders, O.J. invited Paula to a huge fund-raiser thrown by the Pediatric Aids Foundation. That weekend Kato had his daughter Tiffany. He volunteered to baby-sit for all the kids while O.J. and Paula went to the party. That afternoon, Paula showed up in her new Bronco. O.J. suggested she take the kids out for new shoes. Tiffany and Kato went along. It was one of the few occasions when Kato actually spent any significant time with Paula.

She bought the kids new outfits. They were gone a long time, and when they got back, O.J. rushed out of the house and told Paula to hurry or they'd be late. Kato said he'd see them later, and was about to take Tiffany to his room, when O.J. said, "No, you're coming along, man! The kids, too!"

Kato was "stunned." He told O.J. he had nothing to wear and felt like a slob. O.J. told him not to worry, he looked great. A little while later they all found themselves in O.J.'s Bronco, pulling into the famous Robert Taylor ranch in Mandeville Canyon. The place was so big that when they parked, a van had to come and pick them up.

The event was being hosted by Paul Michael Glaser and his AIDS-afflicted wife, Elizabeth. O.J. was running a celebrity booth, playing a carny barker: "See how many pins you can knock down. . . ."

During the course of the evening, Kato was introduced to several celebrities, including Robin Williams, Jon Lovitz, Danny DeVito, Henry Winkler, Mike Meyers, Jay Leno, Anne Archer, Jimmy Connors, Tom Hanks, Michael Douglas, Laura Dern, Elle MacPherson. And Marcus Allen, whom he already knew. "It struck me funny," Kato recalled, "that no matter how big someone was, when they looked at me, they seemed to be trying to figure out who I was and if they were supposed to know me."

At one point during the evening, Kato noticed a bit of tension flare up between Paula and O.J. over some girl at the party he'd once gone out with. O.J. didn't pay any attention to the woman, but it bothered Paula and she decided to let him know it.

O.J. took Kato aside to complain about Paula's attitude. He said he didn't want her interfering with his duties for the evening, which included mingling with people. He couldn't help it, he said, if he "knew" some of the women there.

However, that wasn't the end of it. Penelope Ann Miller, an actress friend of Kato's, showed up with her boyfriend at the time, Gary, also a friend of Kato's. Penelope and Kato chatted for a few minutes, and then he introduced her to Tiffany, who'd gotten all excited when she'd recognized the movie star.

Kato then introduced O.J. to Penelope. After she left, O.J. took him aside and asked how he knew her. Kato told him he'd met her at a dinner party, and they'd hit it off and become friends. "I could tell O.J. was attracted to her. He mentioned to me that he might even like to go out with her sometime.

A little while later, while O.J. and Paula were greeting people under one of the tents, Penny happened to come by. O.J. smiled at her and said, "Hey, isn't this a coincidence. We meet again." He was about to introduce Paula, when suddenly Paula threw her arms around Penny's boyfriend. As it happened, he was a model and knew Paula from a job they'd both worked on.

As they hugged, O.J. pulled Kato aside and asked him about the guy. When Kato told O.J. that Gary was a really cool guy, O.J. frowned, shook his head, and walked away.

As they were getting ready to leave, someone called Paula "Miss Roberts." O.J. started laughing, but Paula failed to see the humor in it and fumed all during the van ride back to the car.

It was late in the day when they finally returned to Rockingham. Kato had to get Tiffany back to his ex-wife, and O.J. had to get Sydney and Justin back to Nicole. Not long after they pulled into the Ashford gate, Paula left in her Bronco.

O.J. was not in the best of moods when he turned to Kato

and said, "Let's get something to eat. We'll take the kids and go to Sizzler's." So there they were, Sunday night in Brentwood, standing in line at a packed family-style restaurant with three restless, hungry, tired children, like everyone else, waiting for a table.

They finally got one, and as soon as they sat down, people started coming over to get O.J.'s autograph. One fellow came by and overstayed his welcome, talking to O.J. for what seemed like the whole dinner. Kato remembered how O.J. "just continued to smile and nod. I could tell, though, that his mood was slowly beginning to darken."

After dinner, Kato had to bring Tiffany home and told O.J. he'd see him later. O.J. grunted and took Sydney and Justin back to Nicole's. "I caught hell from my wife and O.J. did from Nicole as well. Here we were, I thought to myself, two big-shot bachelors of the world, getting shit from our exes for bringing the kids home late."

Still later that night, according to Kato, O.J. had a visit from a Raiderette, which cheered him up considerably.

"About a week before the murders, I was taking my car for a fill-up to a station on San Vicente," he said, "when I drove past Starbucks and saw Nicole sitting there with a couple of girlfriends having coffee. I knew she was still angry at me. I decided to turn around and head in the other direction, hoping she hadn't seen me.

"I suddenly felt sad. We had been so close until I'd moved in with O.J. Did she mean to tell me that if I moved out we'd be friends again? Was that the measure of what we had meant to each other? Maybe she just didn't want to be my friend at all." He told himself that he was going to resolve this situation once and for all, the first chance he got.

Unfortunately, that chance never came. It was the last time Kato saw Nicole alive.

6

To Trial, to Trial

"With the trial approaching, it's been a shark-fest. Everybody's feeding off me. People are making money directly and directly off Nicole, Ron Goldman, O.J., people who have nothing to do with the trial. I think it's just a shame. Maybe it's their last gasp."

—Brian "Kato" Kaelin,
From an interview with
Marc Eliot, February 26, 1995

Not long before the trial,

Brian "Kato" Kaelin received $50,000 to appear on a tabloid show. He no longer had to wait on line to get into clubs. Every day new invitations to the hottest Hollywood parties arrived. Model parties, fragrance parties, parties for parties' sake.

People he never met before greeted him like an old friend. They insisted on buying him drinks, dinners, slipping him passes to shows, sending cars for him, fixing him up with gorgeous women. Beverly Hills and Sunset Boulevard club bartenders began serving "Katos"—vodkas with orange juice on ice. He was wined and dined up and down Rodeo Drive. He played baseball every Saturday morning with his new pal, movie star Charlie Sheen. He was invited to Peter Bogdanovich's birthday party. He went swimming in Malibu. "I went to this one superstar's house, and when I walked in, everyone's head turned to look at me. What a trip! I couldn't believe how everyone knew who I was and wanted their picture taken with me. *Everybody!*"

He was invited, along with Juliette Lewis and Tom Sizemore, to be a celebrity judge for a Halloween bash at American Bar in Santa Monica. The winner, someone who came as "Kato," went home a hundred dollars richer.

He became a fixture in Jay Leno's *Tonight Show* comedy monologue. "Kato Kaelin hopes to get on the jury of the O.J. case. He could use the free room and board!" David Letterman regularly featured him on the "Top Ten" list. One night during his opening monologue, Letterman held up a book he said was from his private collection, entitled *How to Live in Los Angeles on Absolutely Nothing a Day,* by Kato Kaelin. *Saturday Night Live* parodied him in several sketches, one of which named him the perfect next husband for model/actress Cindy Crawford.

Playboy magazine offered to do an interview and put him on the cover. *Vanity Fair* wanted to do a piece on him. Annie Liebovitz photographed him for *The New Yorker.* His every move seemed to be noted in magazines like *Entertainment Weekly* and *People. Esquire* included him in its annual "Dubious Achievements" year-end issue. By that time nearly two dozen features had been done about him in every major magazine in the country.

Larry King invited him to lunch at the Beverly Wilshire Hotel. "Do you realize," Larry asked, "what kind of an impact you've had on everyone? You've become an instant celebrity. If I had the president watching his wife debate Lady Di and I said you just walked in the room, I'd have to say, 'Excuse me, Kato's here, can I put him on?' and they would say, 'Yes, and can we stay and watch?'"

Early in 1995 he met with Barbara Walters in her suite at the Peninsula Hotel in Beverly Hills and eventually sat for an interview with her for *20/20.* NBC's *Dateline* ran a segment called "The Kato Phenomenon." The TV tabs had a field day.

"Fan mail" piled up at the DA's office. Many of the envelopes contained checks from well-wishers saying they wanted to help him out. An autograph dealer approached him with the idea of selling his signature, claiming he could get seventy-five dollars each time he signed his name to a piece of paper. He was invited to appear at the Santa Barbara Film Festival, alongside Jessica Lange.

Strangers in bars told him he ought to run for office. Women sent him provocative photos of themselves, asking if they could come and visit, promising the kind of fun he wouldn't soon forget. He received long, detailed letters explaining why O.J. had to be innocent. Radio shows called from all over the country, asking him to come on, say hello or make an ID for them. Rick Dees recorded a song parody about him for his morning show, based on the hit "I'm Too Sexy for My Shirt." Howard Stern talked about him on the air every day.

The owners of health clubs, restaurants, and clothing stores gave him free memberships and passes, and asked him to stop by so they could take special care of his needs. His name appeared in the Doonesbury cartoon strip.

At a restaurant one night, he got up to go to the men's room, and while he was standing at the urinal, a fellow came up and said, "I'm sorry to bother you, but I'm from *People* magazine. . . . "

Women have chased him down hallways screaming, "Do me, do me. . . . "

He agreed to an interview with a TV reporter from Milwaukee, and flew home like Caesar returning to Rome. Although his plane arrived at two in the morning, there were TV crews waiting for him. The Rams happened to be playing Green Bay that weekend. The president of the team, John Shaw, invited him to see the game from his personal box. He stayed at the same hotel as the team. In the lobby, so many people came over to him that Shaw laughed and jokingly asked him to please leave, because he was making the players feel neglected! At the game, the announcer acknowledged his presence over the stadium sound system, to a thunderous round of applause.

He got a job on a film that was shooting one Thursday night in downtown Los Angeles. The TV tabloids got a hold of the news, and he was mobbed. The next evening, *Entertainment Tonight* ran a feature about the shoot, focused entirely on him.

He was invited to meet with representatives of the top entertainment agencies. He made appearances in feature films, TV sitcoms, and talk shows. He hosted an episode of *Talk Soup*. He drew crowds at the opening of malls. He signed with one of the world's most powerful public-relations firms. He was invited to Washington and black-tied with congressmen. He worked on a Las Vegas–style nightclub comedy act. He sold his services—"coffee with Kato"—for twenty-five dollars a pop, Kato T-shirt included. He had bodyguards. He was the newest phee-nom; this year's Buttafuoco. America's favorite houseguest.

And then he testified.

Among his most striking omissions on the witness stand were two stories he related to me during our time together. One came out as a result of my asking him to find photos for our book. His friends at the time still included, curiously, Cora Fischman, whom he visited one night. The next day, Kato told me in an obviously shaken manner, what he described as a story from a woman who was terribly upset.

Cora told Kato that about a week before the murders, and just after Nicole and O.J. had one of their blowouts, she had a very troubling conversation with O.J. According to Kato, Cora told him that O.J. was in one of his furies and said "She [Nicole] isn't going to get away with this. I'm going to take care of her once and for all."

As disturbing was another story Kato said was making the rounds. There had been press reports about a witness who supposedly saw a white Bronco in the vicinity of Nicole's house the night of the murder and copied down the first three letters of its license plate; they were the same as the first three letters on the plates of A.C. Cowling's Bronco. According to published reports, this witness received a death threat. Kato contends that there is another witness who has more to tell about a Bronco in the neighborhood that night but is fearful about coming forward.

One would think that if Kato had an interest in justice, he might have passed these stories on to the prosecution so that the prosecution could track down these stories and so that the fearful witness could be subpoenaed.

What is it about America's lust for the junk food of popular culture that makes someone like Brian "Kato" Kaelin seem such a fast-food feast? What exactly has he done to deserve the mindless adulation of a public hooked on flavor-of-the-month celebrity? There seems too close a link between the privilege of fame that seduced O.J.—if he is guilty, and I believe he is—that convinced him he was somehow above the laws that govern ordinary men, and the special privileges of celebrity bestowed for the moment on Kato. That both O.J. and Kato share an uneasy ongoing association as the result of the deaths of two innocent victims seems to have been over-shadowed by the sheer belligerence of one and the outrageous arrogance of the other.

Nor am I alone in my belief in Simpson's guilt. On at least a half-dozen occasions, Kato, off-tape, told me he believed O.J. had killed both Nicole Brown Simpson and Ron Goldman, and probably had help doing it. Further he expressed fear of a "freed" O.J. revenging his testimonial "betrayal" at the hands of Brian "Kato" Kaelin.

Finally, have we even once seen O.J. Simpson grieve for the death of his wife and her friend? Or Brian "Kato" Kaelin resist the hot seams of fame's black stockings, out of, if nothing else, respect for the woman (and womankind) who befriended and trusted him with her innermost secrets?

What is wrong with a society that sees Brian "Kato" Kaelin as a hero? What comfort do we draw from his labored innocence? Is he really the brightest representation of his generation, the best reflection of its collective virtues? Can his too obvious, avaricious leap into the spotlight seem to anyone just reparation for the lives of two dead human beings and two victimized children? Is there anything redemptive that's been missed in this crudest of opportunistic displays?

As the O.J. Simpson saga drags into its second year, sometimes even fifteen minutes can seem like an awfully long time.